The City of David

# THE CITY OF DAVID a guide to biblical JERUSALEM

**HERSHEL SHANKS**

THE BIBLICAL ARCHAEOLOGY SOCIETY
Washington, D.C.

Library of Congress
Catalog Card Number:
DS109.S495    1973
915.694'4
74—157016
MARC


ISBN: 0-9607092-1-5
© 1973, 1975 by Hershel Shanks


THE BIBLICAL ARCHAEOLOGY SOCIETY
1737 H Street, Northwest
Washington, D.C. 20006

Published in Israel by
Bazak Israel Guidebook Publishers, Ltd.
Tel Aviv

To my parents

# Acknowledgements

I wish to express my indebtedness and gratitude to the following:

To Professor Yigael Yadin, Director, Institute of Archeology, Hebrew University, whose vast scholarship and perspicacious comments on the entire text have been immeasurably helpful.

To Pierre Benoît, O.P., former Directeur of and now Professeur at the Ecole Biblique et Archéologique Française and a pre-eminent scholar in the history and archeology of Jerusalem, who corrected the entire manuscript and unravelled a number of mysteries for me.

To Dan Bahat of the Israel Department of Antiquities and Museums, whose intimate and extensive knowledge of Jerusalem archeology is matched only by his willingness to share it with, and explain it to, novices like myself. This is a far better book for his help.

To the following scholars who read all or part of the manuscript and saved me from a number of blunders: Dr. Avraham Biran, Director of the Israel Department of Antiquities and Museums; Dr. William G. Dever, Director of the William F. Albright Institute of Archeological Research; and Professor Nachman Avigad of the Institute of Archeology, Hebrew University.

Final judgments on questionable matters have been mine, and the kindness of those people who reviewed my work should not be read as agreement with all of my judgments. The responsibility for the inevitable remaining errors is also mine.

The pictures by Zev Radovan were taken especially for this book. He spared no effort in getting just the right angle at just the right time of day.

The reconstruction of the gateway to the Spring Gihon on page 25 is the work of the talented architect to the current excavations at the southern wall of the Temple Mount, Brian Lalor, who made the drawing especially for this book.

The contribution of my wife Judy is more general, but also more pervasive. Whenever the night seems long and the path murky, she is there to help; and I am more grateful than I can say.

Hershel Shanks

Jerusalem
March 1973

# Contents

Introduction     11

THE BACKGROUND

1. Why the Original City of Jerusalem Is Where It Is    15

2. The Jebusite Wall of Jerusalem    23

3. The Jebusite Shaft Bringing the Waters of Gihon into the City    27

4. The Jebusite Shaft and David's Capture of Jerusalem    31

5. Solomon and the Spring Gihon    38

6. Hezekiah's Tunnel and Sennacherib's Siege of Jerusalem    40

7. Hezekiah's Tunnel — Its Features and Modern Discovery    49

8. Remaining Questions and Some New Answers    63

9. Gihon and Siloam in Later History    75

THE TOUR

1. The Spring Gihon 77

2. The Jebusite Wall 79

3. The Top of the Jebusite Shaft 82

4. The So-Called Tower of David, Nehemiah's Wall and 7th Century B.C.E. Israelite Homes Destroyed in the Babylonian Destruction 84

5. The Underground Tunnel Systems — From the Time of the Jebusites, King Solomon and King Hezekiah 89

6. The Pool of Siloam and The Mosque 95

7. The King's Garden, The Old Pool, The Rock-Cut Scarp and Solomon's Irrigation Channel 97

8. The Tombs Attributed to the Kings of Judah, The Stairway of David, The Synagogue Inscription and The Tower of Siloam 99

9. The Spring of En Rogel 109

Notes 111

Jerusalem Chronology 121

Chronology of Explorations on the Hill of Ophel (The City of David) 123

Suggested Further Reading 126

List of Illustrations 127

# Introduction

This is a guide to some of the most exciting and significant remains of ancient Jerusalem — Jerusalem of the Bible. The Jebusite wall dating from 1800 B.C.E., which David repaired and used as his city wall when he captured Jerusalem from the Jebusites; the Jebusite watershaft through which King David was able to capture the city; the mysterious waters of the Spring Gihon which gush forth intermittently and beside whose flow King Solomon was anointed; the irrigation channel which King Solomon built to water his royal garden; King Hezekiah's tunnel, that miracle of ancient technology by which the wise Hezekiah withstood the siege of Sennacherib; tombs attributed to the kings of Judah; Israelite homes destroyed by the Babylonians during the first destruction of Jerusalem; the city wall built by Nehemiah on the exiles' return; a Maccabean tower built to defend the city in Hasmonean times — all this and more are described in detail for the first time in a guidebook. Indeed, this is the only guidebook devoted to the City of David on the hill of Ophel, which lies outside the present old city walls.

These remains are exciting not only for what they are, but also because they call upon the traveler to reason and understand, not just to look. True, there are some sites described here, the facts of which you will have to accept on faith. For example, you will see some 7th century B.C.E. Israelite homes which were destroyed by the Babylonians. You will not be able to confirm on your own the date of these houses; even a trained scholar could not do that unless he had available to him the pottery sherds that were associated with the wall when it was excavated. But there is much in this book that you *can* reason out for yourself. By examining these remains with the background provided here, you will understand why the City of David was located where it was, how a tradition of centuries as to its location on Mount Zion was proved wrong, why the life-giving spring that called the city of Jerusalem into being was not included within its walls. From evidence which you yourself can examine, you will understand how Hezekiah's great tunnel was built, when the two crews of tunnelers began to hear the blows of each other's pick-axes, how and where they met.

You will also participate in a century of archeological exploration. You will understand how an archeologist who thought he had found the tower of David was proved wrong. You will understand how the archeologist who in 1961 found the Jebusite city wall chose the right spot to dig. You will share the archeologist's dismay at finding that Hezekiah's tunnel led the water from one point outside the city wall to another point outside the city wall. You will understand how this problem may have been solved in 1970 by an archeologist digging in the Jewish Quarter of the present walled city of Jerusalem.

Finally, these remains are exciting because they relate to specific historical incidents described in the Bible. Frequently archeology provides only a background for a biblical period. It helps us to understand the people and how they lived. But sometimes, as is the case with much of the remains described here, archeology illuminates specific biblical incidents. These incidents are described here in the context of the archeological materials used to enlighten them — David's conquest of Jerusalem; Solomon's throne saved from his usurping brother, Adonijah; Sennacherib's siege of Jerusalem.

Why, the reader may ask, if these sites are so exciting, have they been so generally ignored by tourists. It is true that until 1967 they were not available to the tourist visiting Israel. But that is not the whole reason. There is another reason, and that is that these remains require understanding and background. They require the tourist to bring his intelligence to them. The very thing that makes them exciting also places them beyond the interest of many tourists.

Some tourist sites hit you between the eyes. I think of the Taj Mahal in India, the Acropolis in Athens, Persepolis in southern Iran or Masada in the Judean desert. Appreciation of such sites is immediate and direct. Of course, the more you understand of their histories and the cultures that lie behind them, the deeper is your appreciation. But people with almost no understanding travel half-way round the world to see these sites — and justifiably so — simply for the immediate aesthetic impact.

At the other extreme are sites which have almost no meaning unless you know a great deal about what you are looking at. This is true of most, though not all, of the sites described here. Take the Spring Gihon, where we begin our tour. From the road, you would pass it by. If you stop, you would look down some steps to an iron gate beyond which are some more steps leading to a spring. The guide tells you that here Solomon was anointed king and here is the beginning of Hezekiah's tunnel. You get back into the car or bus, and drive on. A world has passed you by.

Take a second look . . .

# The Background

## 1 Why the Original City of Jerusalem Is Where It Is

The Spring Gihon (Fig. 1), which is the first stop on our tour, is the most important factor that accounts for the location of the original pre-Israelite city of Jerusalem about 5000 years ago.

The other factor of course is geography. For Jerusalem lies on a narrow crest in the central part of the country through which all north-south traffic — both commercial and military — passed in ancient times. To the east and west of this crest, known as the watershed line, are deep wadi valleys, leading to the Jordan Valley and the Aravah on the east and to the Mediterranean Sea on the west. To travel in a north-south direction up and down these wadi valleys would be incredibly difficult. The only real alternative in the central part of Canaan was to stick to the central crest. At Jerusalem the crest narrows and takes a short east-west turn. The city lies astride this narrow gap between the deep wadi valleys. This central route

Fig. 1. The entrance to the water tunnel at the Spring Gihon.

was especially important when, as was often the case, the ancient Mediterranean coastal route (known as the Via Maris) was in the hands of a hostile people like the Philistines, and the route along the plateau east of the Jordan River (known as the King's Highway) was controlled by alien groups like the Ammonites, the Moabites and the Edomites. When these routes were unavailable, Jerusalem lay on the geographical bridge between Egypt and Mesopotamia to the east.

There are a number of hills on this watershed crest near the site of Jerusalem (such as the Temple Mount on which Solomon was later to build his temple), but two of these hills have special advantages as an ancient city site. These two hills, known today as Mount Zion and the hill of Ophel[1], are ridges or spurs which jut south of the main watershed crest, just below the present walled city (Fig. 2). Each of these ridges or spurs (Zion and Ophel) is surrounded on three sides by deep natural valleys which make them easily defensible, except on their northern side. On the east is an almost vertical slope down to the Kidron Valley, which provides a better defense than man could build. On the west is the equally deep, if slightly less steep, Hinnom Valley which curves around on the south to meet the Kidron. Between the two ridges is the Tyropoean Valley, another natural defense against attack[2]. These three valleys gave the two ridges their special advantages as ancient city sites, and explain why the choice of the original town site of Jerusalem was confined by geography to either the western ridge (Zion) or the eastern ridge (Ophel).

As a town site, however, the western ridge (Zion) has many advantages over the eastern ridge (Ophel). In the first place, Mount Zion is much larger and broader. Because it is also flatter and less sloping, it is much easier to build on, with far less need for retaining walls than the narrow, steeply-sloped hill of Ophel. The western ridge is also higher than the eastern ridge by almost 240 feet. In summer, the western ridge faces a cool western breeze.

With all these advantages, the western ridge would appear to be the obvious choice for the first town site of Jerusalem. And indeed the almost unanimous opinion of scholars until the end of the 19th century was that the original city of Jerusalem, which we now know goes back to about 3000 B.C.E., as well as the City of David, was located on the western ridge. Certainly this location was confirmed by tradition[3]. Ever since men could remember, the western ridge was known as Mount Zion, and even today that is its name. There, also, the traditional tomb of King David is located. The western ridge as the original city's location is confirmed by common sense as well. Those early explorers who suggested that the original city and the City of David were located on the eastern ridge, the hill of Ophel, were met with scholarly derision. Why would the original builders of Jerusalem choose as the site of their city the smallest and the lowest hill in the area, especially when they had available the western ridge with all its advantages.

Of course the scholars were all wrong.

Gradually excavations of the defenses on the eastern ridge (and the water systems which we shall shortly discuss) convinced even the most recalcitrant scholars — tradition to the contrary notwithstanding — that the original city site and the City of David were located not on what we call Mount Zion, but on the little eastern ridge known as Ophel*. Today it is unanimously

---

* Because so many visitors to Jerusalem are surprised by the fact, it is necessary to emphasize that Jerusalem during King David's reign did not extend to any portion of the present walled city of Jerusalem. King Solomon extended David's city northward

agreed that the original city of Jerusalem and the City of David were confined exclusively to the eastern ridge, or the hill of Ophel[4].

Why did the Jebusites, a Canaanite people[5] who built a city here before the Israelites[6], choose the less attractive eastern ridge, despite all the advantages of the western ridge? The reason is the Spring Gihon.

The Spring Gihon lies on the eastern slope of the eastern ridge (Fig. 6). It is the only defensible ancient spring in the area, and for that reason Gihon determined the location of the city of Jerusalem[7]. Immediate access to a spring was vitally important in Jebusite times because the Jebusites had no effective cisterns. Not until King David's time (c. 1000 B.C.E.) or perhaps 100 years earlier was lime plaster extensively used. The invention of lime plaster was a major contribution to civilization because with it cisterns could be employed anywhere that water could be carried. The lime plaster could be used to line a large hole and store water almost indefinitely[8]. But the Jebusites had no lime plaster cisterns. They were dependent on living water. If they did not have immediate access to a live spring, they would be vulnerable to siege which would soon thirst them out[9]; and that is why the Spring Gihon on the eastern slope of the hill of Ophel determined the location of Jerusalem.

The Spring Gihon is located in a cave. You will see this natural cave as you enter the second set of

---

to the present Temple Mount area, (see Fig. 11), but not to other areas enclosed by the present city wall. All traditional or popular sites outside of this area and bearing titles like David's Tower or David's Tomb are therefore not actually attributable to David nor to the time in which he lived.

The present location of the old city of Jerusalem, which excludes the City of David, was fixed, with minor exceptions, by the Romans when they built Aelia Capitolina in 135 C.E., from which Jews were excluded. The present wall of the old city was built by Suleiman the Magnificent in 1535 C.E. and follows generally the lines of Aelia Capitolina.

steps going down to the spring. In ancient days the top of this cave was at ground level. The source of the spring lay deep within the earth and gushed forth intermittently throughout the day through cracks in the floor of the cave. It still does. That is why the spring is called Gihon, for Gihon in Hebrew means "gushing". Etymologically, the word suggests something bursting forth suddenly and mysteriously. The intermittent gushes are a result of a peculiar natural subterranean siphon system consisting of a number of interior caverns.

The frequency with which Gihon sends forth its water depends on the amount of rainfall and the season of the year. The gushes last from 30 to 40 minutes and then the water recedes for four to ten hours. The spring also has a small constant flow. In this way, the spring supplies between 7,000 and 40,000 cubic feet of water per day. This was more than enough for the ancient city. Indeed, within the walls water was plenteous, although all was parched outside. Strabo, the ancient Greek geographer, gave an accurate description of the city: "Jerusalem is a rocky well-enclosed fortress, well-watered within, wholly dry without".

The Spring Gihon's intermittent flow which sometimes begins with a loud echoing noise, has given rise to many legends and stories. One pious traveler from the 4th century, known to history only as the Pilgrim of Bordeaux, had a vivid, if holy, imagination when he reported that, "This spring flows six days and six nights, but on the seventh day it is the Sabbath. Then it flows not, neither the whole day nor the whole night".

➤

Fig. 2. Model of the rock contours of Jerusalem showing (2) the eastern ridge (Ophel) and (4) the western ridge (Zion), divided (3) by the Tyropoean Valley, with (1) the Kidron Valley on the east and (5) the Hinnom Valley on the west.

Nehemiah, when he returned to Jerusalem after the Babylonian exile, made a tour by night of the broken down walls of the city. He started near the "Dragon Spring", which was probably the Spring Gihon or an outlet from it (Nehemiah 2:13)[10]. One of the early explorers of Gihon, Edward Robinson, reported in 1838 that the Arabs living about the spring believed that a dragon lived beneath the cave from which the water issued. When the dragon is awake, he stops the water. When he sleeps, it flows. From Nehemiah (c. 445 B.C.E.) to 1838 is a long time, but perhaps this story goes back that far and accounts for the fact that in Nehemiah's time the spring was known as the Dragon Spring.

We shall return to the Spring Gihon, but now let us look at the Jebusite and Davidic wall of Jerusalem, the second stop on our tour.

## 2 The Jebusite Wall of Jerusalem

If you climb the steps leading up the hill from the Spring Gihon about 150 feet and look into the excavations on your right, you will see a line of stones which are the remains of the Jebusite city wall that once enclosed the entire city (Fig. 3). (See section on "Tour" for exact directions.) Pottery found in the foundation trench of this wall indicates that it was built in about 1800 B.C.E. This wall, although often repaired, was used continuously until about the 8th century B.C.E.[11]

This Jebusite wall of Jerusalem was not found by archeologists until 1961, when it was exposed for the first time by one of the most distinguished living biblical archeologists, Miss Kathleen M. Kenyon. How Miss Kenyon happened to excavate for the wall in this location is an interesting story which we shall tell when we look at the remains of what was previously thought to be the Jebusite wall, higher up on the hill. (See the discussion of the so-called "Tower of David" in the "Tour" section.)

As you will see in Fig. 3, the short section of the Jebusite wall that has been excavated contains an angle. This indicated to the excavator either that the wall contained a series of insets or that the angled portion was part of a tower in the wall. When Miss Kenyon discovered later in the excavation that the wall continued north before the end of the angled side of the wall (i.e., the angled side of the wall ran behind the continuation of the wall northward), she concluded that she had hit a tower in the wall. This was

Fig. 3. The lowest wall — with an angle in it — is the Jebusite wall dating from 1800 B.C.E. This wall was still in use when David captured the city in about 993 B.C.E. The angle in the wall was probably part of a gate tower, matched by a similar gate tower on the other side of the gate, to the left (south). The wall directly behind the Jebusite wall was the city wall at the time of the Babylonian destruction. It had been used for about 150 years. The wall behind that is modern terracing.

Fig. 4. A reconstruction of the city gate above the Spring Gihon, the red-shaded part of which was first uncovered in 1961-62 by the British archeologist, Kathleen Kenyon. The shaded part is still **in situ** and may be seen by visitors. In all likelihood, the stone was covered with a mud or lime plaster during most of the period of its use.

probably a gate tower, flanking the ancient city gate which was used by the ordinary people during times of peace to go down to the Spring Gihon for water. To the left (south) of this tower, on the other side of the gate, no doubt stood a complementary tower flanking the gateway. With a little imagination you can visualize how it looked in ancient times, although but a few rocks remain today (Fig. 4).

This Jebusite wall raises an interesting question. Although it surrounded the pre-Davidic city, it lies higher up on the ridge than the Spring Gihon. In short, this all-important water supply lies *outside* the city wall. If the defense of the Spring Gihon was so important, why did the canny Jebusites leave it exposed outside the city wall, instead of including it in the walled city?

To understand why the Jebusites did not place the wall lower on the slope so as to include the Spring Gihon, look further down the slope into the Kidron Valley. If the wall were placed so low on the slope as to include the Spring Gihon, it would be vulnerable to attack by slingstones, javelins, spears and arrows from the other side of the valley. The Jebusites, who were to retain their hold on Jerusalem against the pressure of the Israelite conquest until King David's time, were not so foolish as to build a useless wall so near the foot of the valley.

## 3 The Jebusite Shaft Bringing The Waters of Gihon into the City

But the fact that the Spring Gihon lies outside the city wall did not mean that it was entirely exposed. During time of danger, the entrance to the Spring was covered and camoflaged, which was easily done because its source was buried in a cave. Access to the spring when the city was under attack — and this was crucial — was not by walking outside the wall and dipping a bucket into the spring, but by an underground shaft whose entrance was inside the city wall.

The best known of these shafts is Hezekiah's Tunnel which we shall discuss later at length. But long before Hezekiah built his famous tunnel, the Jebusites had the same idea.

In 1867, Captain Charles Warren, an Englishman who performed some classic excavations and who surveyed Jerusalem for the Palestine Exploration Fund, discovered a shaft, later attributed to the Jebusites[12], leading from inside the city walls, through the rock

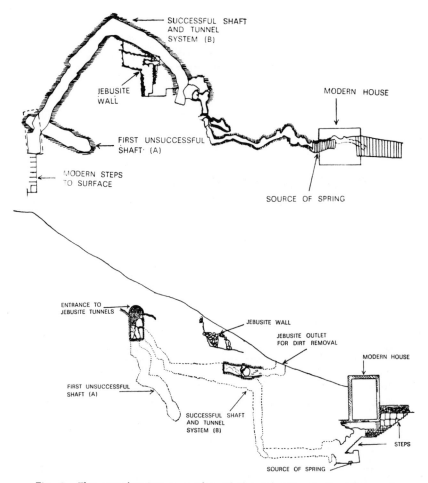

Fig. 5. The top drawing is a plan of the Jebusite shaft and tunnel system used to bring water inside the city during time of siege. Naturally the plan can show no elevations. The major feature of the plan is the semi-circular tunnel leading to the main vertical shaft going down to the Spring Gihon. The bottom drawing is a section drawing of the same Jebusite shaft and tunnel system, which gives, as it were, a side view, as if the mountain had been cut away. Shaft A is the Jebusite's first, unsuccessful attempt to dig a shaft. Apparently they hit hard rock and decided to start a new shaft. The second effort, to the right, was successful. The passage leading up to the ground, to the right of the main shaft, was dug by the Jebusites to enable them to remove the dirt and rock that was dug to create the shaft and tunnel system. After the shaft and tunnel system was completed, this passage was blocked up. Note the Jebusite wall located between the Spring Gihon and the outlet of the shaft and tunnel system, which places this outlet inside the city wall.

beneath, and down into the spring (see Fig. 5). Indeed, he discovered two shafts which began at the same opening inside the city walls. The first shaft went almost straight down, but came to a sudden dead end. Apparently the intention was to go down to the level of the Spring Gihon and connect the shaft with the spring by a tunnel which would convey the water to the bottom of the shaft. Reaching a source of water outside city walls by means of a shaft and tunnel is now a familiar pattern in ancient Israelite and Canaanite cities. The best known of these shafts and tunnels is at Megiddo, but similar shafts and tunnels have also been excavated at Hazor, Gibeon and Gezer. However, at Jerusalem the first Jebusite shaft hit a strata of bedrock so hard that is could not be penetrated with the Jebusites' soft bronze tools* and had to be abandoned. Not easily discouraged, the Jebusites tried a second time, starting from the same point, but working in a different, diagonal direction. Instead of going straight down, they worked at an angle. They built a stair-case down to a platform, which led into a horizontal semi-circular tunnel at a level about half-way down to the spring. At the end of the tunnel is another shaft going further down into the mountain. The bottom of this shaft ends in what was then a water-filled channel which leads to the Spring Gihon (see Fig. 5). In this somewhat zigzag way, the Jebusites hit softer strata of rock and accomplished their mission. By lowering a bucket down the last shaft, the Jebusites could reach the water. The water of the Spring Gihon was at last available to the Jebusites from inside the city walls.

---

* The Iron Age, which follows the Bronze Ages, begins in about 1200 B.C.E. At about that time the Philistines brought to Canaan the secret of iron which they probably learned from the Hittites. The Philistines were careful not to let the Israelites in on the secret. (See I Samuel 13:19-22).

This shaft and tunnel system was vital to the Jebusite defense of the city. Those who have explored it have found evidence of its long and heavy use to bring the waters of Gihon inside the city walls. The steps are rubbed and worn and sometimes cracked with use, and gashes have been carved in the rock where centuries of bucket ropes have been pulled up.

The end of this Jebusite shaft, not to be confused with Hezekiah's Tunnel, may still be seen. (More specific instructions are given in the "Tour" section). From the Spring Gihon, approximately the first 65 feet of the tunnel is the work originally of the Jebusites, although it was later re-worked by Hezekiah (see Fig. 11). As you traverse the tunnel from the Spring Gihon, you will make a 90-degree left hand turn after the first 65 feet. It is at this left hand turn that the later tunnel of Hezekiah begins, and you will notice that it is of a much higher calibre workmanship than the first 65 feet of tunnel. If you were to go straight ahead instead of turning left into Hezekiah's Tunnel, you would continue into the Jebusite tunnel and be able to look up the Jebusite shaft. However, the way is now blocked to all but the most agile, though there is a small hole through which you can see where the bottom of the Jebusite shaft connects with the channel bringing the Gihon waters to the shaft. The other end of the Jebusite shaft and tunnel system (from inside the city walls) is now covered, although a tunnel leading to the stopped-up entrance can be seen.

Perhaps some day the Jebusite shaft will be cleared so that it will be more accessible to visitors*.

---

* Over 100 years ago, Captain Warren expressed the intention of clearing the Jebusite shaft so that visitors could see this water system more easily. Unfortunately, he never got around to it; however, it would not be difficult to do so.

# 4 The Jebusite Shaft and David's Capture of Jerusalem

The Jebusite city of Jerusalem — surrounded by a wall — occupied less than 11 acres (see Fig. 6 for an outline of the city at the time of David). It is hard to think of a more significant 11 acres of ancient Israel. In the hands of the Jebusites, Jerusalem was like a wall dividing the Israelites in half. And, interestingly enough, when the country split apart after King Solomon's death (c. 922 B.C.E.), the dividing line was at Jerusalem, with Israel comprising the land to the north, and Judah (including the Jerusalem area) the land to the south.

The biblical record is clear that during the period of the Israelite conquest of Canaan the Israelites fully appreciated the importance of Jerusalem, wanted very much to take it from the Jebusites, and were unsuccessful in doing so. The early alliance of five Amorite kings who fought Joshua at Gibeon included the king of Jerusalem. Joshua defeated them all when the sun stood still at Gibeon, thus giving Joshua a full 24 hours of daylight to complete his task. Joshua captured the kings and hung each of them, including the king of Jerusalem (Joshua 10). But carefully enough, the biblical text makes no claim that Joshua took possession of Jerusalem. Then comes the explicit admission: "But the people of Judah could not drive out the Jebusites, the inhabitants of Jerusalem; so the Jebusites dwell with the people of Judah at Jerusalem to this day" (Joshua 15:63).

Judah had another go at Jerusalem during the period of the Judges after the death of Joshua. According to the biblical record, Judah conquered the city (Judges 1:8), but either the biblical account is exaggerated or the conquerors were not able to hold the city. For shortly thereafter (Judges 1:21) we learn that the Benjaminites, within whose territory Jerusalem lay, "did not drive out the Jebusites that inhabited Jerusalem". Later references to Jerusalem as a city of foreigners where a Levite should not spend the night (Judges 19) confirm this interpretation of the biblical account, which, however, is most convincingly substantiated by the account of David's capture of the city much later (c. 993 B.C.E.) — seven years after he became king (2 Samuel 5:1-9).

David's capture of Jerusalem was by no means assured. The strength of the Jebusite fortress is reflected in the fact that Saul, the first king of Israel, apparently made no attempt to capture the city even though his own capital at Gibeah was just three miles north of the Jebusite city. After resisting Israelite pressure for over 200 years, the Jebusites were apparently so confident that David's attack would be unsuccessful that they taunted David with the cry that even the lame and the blind could defend the city against him (2 Samuel 5:6).

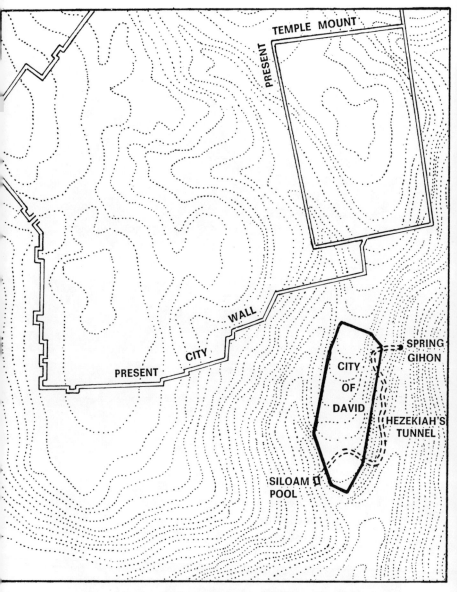

Fig. 6. The city of Jerusalem in King David's time. Hezekiah's tunnel was not, of course, in existence then, but is included on the plan together with contemporary landmarks to orient the reader.

The story of David's capture of the city is told in two places in the Bible, once in 2 Samuel 5:6-9 and again in 1 Chronicles 11:4-7*. The text is difficult and in many places corrupt[13], but putting the two accounts together in their most likely meaning it appears that this is the story: The Jebusites taunted David that the lame and the blind could defend the city, and perhaps the Jebusites even placed the lame and the blind on the city walls as make-believe defenders. David reacted by offering to appoint as commander of his army the man who would first smite the Jebusites and get up the watershaft. Joab was successful in doing this, and, as a result, David captured the city and made Joab commander of his army. Jerusalem thenceforth became the City of David.

The Hebrew word which I have translated "watershaft" is "tsinnor". While watershaft is its most probable meaning, many other meanings have been proposed, some by unusually eminent scholars[14]. The New

---

* The text of these two passages (from the Revised Standard Version) is as follows :

And the king and his men went to Jerusalem against the Jebusites, the inhabitants of the land, who said to David, "You will not come in here, but the blind and the lame will ward you off" — thinking, "David cannot come in here". Nevertheless David took the stronghold of Zion, that is, the City of David. And David said on that day, "Whoever would smite the Jebusites, let him get up the watershaft to attack the lame and the blind, who are hated by David's soul." . . . And David dwelt in the stronghold and called it the City of David (2 Samuel 5:6-9).

And David and all Israel went to Jerusalem, that is, Jebus, where the Jebusites were, the inhabitants of the land. The inhabitants of Jebus said to David, "You will not come in here". Nevertheless David took the stronghold of Zion, that is, the City of David. David said, "Whoever shall smite the Jebusites first shall be chief and commander." And Joab the son of Zeruiah went up first, so he became chief. And David dwelt in the stronghold; therefore it was called the City of David (I Chronicles 11:4-7).

◄

Fig. 7. A rare picture inside the Jebusite tunnel, taken during the Parker Mission, 1909—1911. See also Fig. 24.

English Bible translates the word "grappling hooks", suggesting that the word refers to the grappling hooks that were used to scale the city walls[15]. One reputable scholar contends that the word really means "penis", and suggests that the man who was to be named army commander was required to maim the Jebusites in that vital organ, just as the Jebusites taunted the Israelites that the maimed blind and lame could defend the city — a kind of poetic justice. However, Aquila in his 2d century C.E. Greek translation of the Bible translates the word as "watercourse" and the King James Version translates it as "gutter". These translations were made at a time when the translators had no idea of the existence of the Jebusite watershaft. Combined with the archeological and philological evidence, a strong case has been made that "tsinnor" refers to the Jebusite watershaft that may still be found on the hill of Ophel.

But even if we accept the translation of "tsinnor" as watershaft, that does not end the difficulties. Some scholars argue that David's plan of attack was to get inside the city's almost impregnable defenses by climbing up the watershaft. To anyone who has examined the Jebusite channels, it is clear that to ascend the shaft from the Spring Gihon would be an extremely difficult task — but not, as some have argued, an impossible one. To prove it can be done, one of the staff members — a particularly hardy fellow — of the Parker Mission, which explored the hill of Ophel in 1909-1911, did it. According to the report of their investigation, "All Joab had to do before getting into the tunnel was to wait for a propitious moment ... Some planks of wood, properly arranged by the help of one or two plucky companions, were enough to hoist Joab to the top of the vertical chimney."[16]

Other scholars who accept the reference to "tsinnor" as watershaft argue that David conquered the city not by getting up the watershaft, but by discovering and capturing the Jebusite water source. Once this was done, the Israelites were in a position to deny the city water. According to this theory, thirst, despondency and finally surrender followed.

Thus it appears that in one way or another, the Jebusite watershaft played a crucial role in David's conquest of Jerusalem[17]. Once conquered, the city belonged to David alone. It was not part of any tribe's territory. With a stroke of political genius, he made it his new capital, the City of David.

There he reigned for 33 tumultuous years. David's Jerusalem was, the archeologists tell us, the same geographically as the Jebusite city. For his defenses, he used the Jebusite wall, although, as the Bible suggests, he made repairs in it (2 Samuel 5:9)[18]. Not until Solomon's time did the city expand northward to part of the present walled city and Temple Mount (Fig. 15).

## 5  Solomon and the Spring Gihon

When David was an old man and close to death,
his son Adonijah attempted to seize his throne. Adonijah took his followers outside the city and held a
great coronation feast for himself beside the spring
of En Rogel, another stop on our tour. However, David
had promised that Solomon, his already wise son,
would succeed him. When David heard that Adonijah
was having himself crowned king at En Rogel, David
from his death bed directed Nathan the prophet and
Zadok the priest to put his son Solomon on David's
mule and to take Solomon with the people to the
place of anointing where they were to anoint him king.
Thus the throne was saved for Solomon. The exciting
story is told in 1 Kings 1.

The Bible gives no explanation as to why David
directed Nathan the prophet and Zadok the priest to
take Solomon to the particular place David chose for the
anointing. But the place is identified with certainty:
Gihon. Perhaps the old king recalled that it was by the

capture of the Spring Gihon that he was able to take Jerusalem and thereby, for a time, forge Israel into a unified country. Or perhaps Gihon's intermittently gushing waters were considered sacred even then. Or perhaps the life-giving waters of the spring represented to the dying old king the continuity of Israel and its God:

> *So Zadok the priest and Nathan the prophet... went down and mounted Solomon on King David's mule, and escorted him to Gihon. There Zadok the priest took the horn of oil from the Tent of the Lord, and anointed Solomon. Then they blew the ram's horn, and all the people shouted, "Long live King Solomon!" Then all the people went up after him in procession, playing on pipes, and rejoicing with great joy, so that the very earth was split with the noise (1 Kings 1:38-40).*

The gate through which the procession entered the city after this joyous coronation was, it has been suggested, the gate uncovered by Miss Kenyon in 1961 (see Fig. 4).

# 6 Hezekiah's Tunnel and Sennacherib's Siege of Jerusalem

From the accession of Solomon (c. 961 B.C.E.) to the time of King Hezekiah (c. 715 B.C.E.) is almost 250 years, a time of triumph and tragedy for Israel. After King Solomon's death (c. 922 B.C.E.), the united kingdom disintegrated. The ten northern tribes formed the kingdom of Israel and rejected the Davidic dynasty. David's line continued to rule in the south — the kingdom of Judah — for another 300 years. Though there were bad kings and good kings, bad times and good times, the glories of David and Solomon were never to return. And the long-term trend of events was against these tiny monarchies; the little kingdoms of Israel and Judah became mere pawns in the game of international political chess. Often they were hardly more than vassels to the major political power, who-ever that happened to be. During the 8th century most of the then-known world was under the domination of Assyria, which, in 722 B.C.E., completed the conquest and destruction of the northern kingdom, Israel. An unbelievably cruel people, even for the ancient world, the Assyrians deported most of the upper classes of Israel, and other peoples were settled in their place (see Fig. 8). The Israelites of the northern kingdom were never to reassemble as a people. To history they

Fig. 8. A detail of the low-relief, stone-carved panel installed by Sennacherib in his palace at Nineveh, showing Judean captives impaled on Assyrian spears and carried aloft, apparently in a victory procession. A copy of this panel may be seen in the Israel Museum.

are known as the ten lost tribes. Those who were deported were never heard from again; those who remained intermarried with the new local population and became the Samaritans, a small group of which survives to this day at Nablus and Holon.

Judah, the southern kingdom, was also under Assyrian pressure. Judah watched with increasing anxiety as a parade of Assyrian kings with fearsome names — Tiglath-Pileser, Shalmanesser, Sargon, and Sennacherib — expanded their kingdoms on an obvious path of world conquest. Assyrian advances were stopped only by the need to mend internal fences at home or a change of kings which required a period of consolidation. After the fall of the northern kingdom, the Assyrians advanced down the Mediterranean coast all the way to the Egyptian border.

When Hezekiah (c. 715-687 B.C.E.) came to the throne, Judah was already paying tribute to the Assyrians, although internally Judah prospered under his rule. Hezekiah was one of the few kings in the divided kingdom whom the biblical historians find wholly praiseworthy for "he did what was right in the eyes of the Lord, according to all that David his father had done" (2 Kings 18:3; 2 Chronicles 29:2). Among other things, he cleaned and repaired the Temple. Hezekiah was even successful militarily. He drove the Philistines in the southwest back into the coastal area along the Mediterranean. Doubtless encouraged by this success, Hezekiah, in alliance with Egypt, decided to attempt to throw off the yoke of Assyria and refused to pay tribute. Apparently for a time he was successful in defying the power of Assyria. But Hezekiah's little mountain kingdom of Judah was hardly a match for the military might of the Assyrian hordes, once assembled. Assyrian attack was inevitable and when it came, it burst forth with terrifying force.

42

A number of Judean cities — 46 according to Assyrian records unearthed by the archeologists — including Gibeah and Beth Shemesh, were destroyed by the new Assyrian king Sennacherib, and many more became his vassals. Then in 701 B.C.E. Sennacherib in a swift campaign destroyed the great Judean city of Lachish. Hezekiah sued for peace. He agreed to pay Sennacherib whatever tribute he imposed if he would withdraw from the land. Hezekiah stripped the silver and gold from the Temple to raise booty for the Assyrian king. But even this did not result in an Assyrian withdrawal (2 Kings 18:13-16). Flushed with victory, Sennacherib laid siege to Hezekiah's capital, Jerusalem[19].

In this context, Isaiah the prophet, who had advised against alliance with Egypt[20], inveighed against the land, with some of the most powerful words a prophet ever used:

*O sinful nation, people loaded with iniquity ...*
*Your country is desolate, your cities lie in ashes;*
*Strangers devour your land before your eyes ...*
*Only Zion [Jerusalem] is left ...*
*Your countless sacrifices, what are they to me?*
*    says the Lord.*
*I am sated with the whole-offerings of rams and*
*    the fat of buffaloes ...*
*Though you offer countless prayers,*
*I will not listen ...*
*Put away the evil of your deeds,*
*    away out of my sight.*
*Cease to do evil and learn to do right,*
*Pursue justice and champion the oppressed;*
*Give the orphan his rights, plead the widows'*
*    cause ...*
*Then though your sins are scarlet,*
*They may become white as snow ...*
*Then I will secure a respite from my foes*
*and take vengeance on my enemies ...*

*Then ... you shall be called*
*the home of righteousness, the faithful city.*
*Justice shall redeem Zion [Jerusalem]*
*and righteousness her repentent people (Isaiah 1).*

Although, as the prophet said, only Jerusalem was left, Sennacherib's siege of Jerusalem was unsuccessful and Hezekiah's kingdom was saved. We do not know how long the siege lasted before it broke; nor is it entirely clear what broke it. Did the people repent and do justice in response to the prophet's admonition? At one point, the Bible suggests that in answer to Hezekiah's prayer the Lord slew in a single night 185,000 Assyrians encamped outside Jerusalem (2 Kings 19:35). As a direct result, Sennacherib suddenly gave up the siege and returned home. Based on this biblical suggestion, those who like to give naturalistic explanations for biblical miracles have opined that perhaps a plague hit the Assyrian camp. Support for this suggestion comes from the Greek historian, Herodotus, who reports in his history that the Assyrians were overrun by a horde of mice or rats, which suggests the bubonic plague[21]. On the other hand, the Bible itself contains a suggestion that Sennacherib heard a rumor which caused him to return (2 Kings 19:7). Perhaps rumors of internal dissension, which periodically beset Assyrian rulers, required — or, at least, **was** thought to require — Sennacherib's sudden and prompt return. In any event, the Assyrian hordes departed and Jerusalem was saved.

For much of this ancient story, we have unusual contemporaneous extra-biblical confirmation. Archeologists have unearthed three cuneiform prisms which recount in the first person the accomplishments of Sennacherib's reign. This is what they say:

> *As to Hezekiah, the Judahite, he did not submit*
> *to my yoke. I laid siege to 46 of his strong cities,*

Fig. 9. A cuneiform prism recounting in the first person Sennacherib's military campaign against Hezekiah and his kingdom of Judah, in which Sennacherib boasts of having conquered 46 Judean cities and of having made Hezekiah a prisoner in Jerusalem, "like a bird in a cage". The original of this prism may be seen at the Israel Museum in Jerusalem.

*walled forts and to countless small villages in their vicinity and conquered them by means of earth-ramps and battering rams combined with an attack by foot soldiers. I drove out over 200,000 people, young and old, male and female, horses, mules, donkeys, camels, big and small cattle beyond counting, and considered them booty. [Hezekiah] I made a prisoner in Jerusalem, his royal residence, like a bird in a cage (Fig. 9).*

Hezekiah may have been in a cage, but Sennacherib was not able to break inside the cage and, pointedly enough, Sennacherib does not claim that he was able to conquer Jerusalem.

I cannot refrain from re-printing a thrilling — though much later — recounting of the story: Lord Byron's romantic "Destruction of Sennacherib", which he wrote in 1815:

*The Assyrian came down like a wolf on the fold,*
*And his cohorts were gleaming in purple and gold;*
*And the sheen of their spears was like stars on the sea,*
*When the blue wave rolls nightly on deep Galilee.*
*Like the leaves of the forest when Summer is green,*
*That host with their banners at sunset were seen:*
*Like the leaves of the forest when Autumn hath blown,*
*That host on the morrow lay withered and strown.*
*For the Angel of Death spread his wings on the blast,*
*And breathed in the face of the foe as he passed;*
*And the eyes of the sleepers waxed deadly and chill,*
*And their hearts but once heaved, and forever grew still !*
*And there lay the steed with his nostril all wide,*
*But through it there rolled not the breath of his pride;*
*And the foam of his gasping lay white on the turf,*
*And cold as the spray of the rock-beating surf.*
*And there lay the rider distorted and pale,*
*With the dew on his brow, and the rust on his mail:*

*And the tents were all silent — the banners alone —*
*The lances unlifted — the trumpet unblown.*
*And the widows of Ashur are loud in their wail,*
*And the idols are broke in the temple of Baal;*
*And the might of the Gentile, unsmote by the*
*sword,*
*Hath melted like snow in the glance of the Lord!*

Let us return to Hezekiah's defense of Jerusalem during the Assyrian siege, for if this defense had not been as organized and imaginative as it was, Sennacherib's troops might well have been successful before they were forced — for whatever reason — to withdraw.

The Bible tells us that Hezekiah, in preparation for the siege which he saw coming, organized the city militarily and collected a large quantity of weapons and shields. And with words, the Judean king encouraged and inspired his people. In a biblically recorded speech, he addressed them:

> *Be strong; be brave. Do not let the king of Assyria or the rabble he has brought with him strike terror or panic in your hearts. We have more on our side than he has. He has human strength. But we have the Lord our God to help us and to fight our battles (2 Chronicles 32:7-8).*

However, it is evident that Hezekiah did not depend on God alone; he prudently prepared for the siege.

Before the siege, Sennacherib had sent messengers to Jerusalem to deliver a message to Hezekiah's people. The core of the message was this: "Hezekiah is misleading you into risking death by famine and thirst when he tells you that the Lord your God will save you" (2 Chronicles 32:11). It was clear that Sennacherib intended to capture the city by starving out the Jerusalemites and depriving them of water. Thirst was the threat Sennacherib considered to be most fearsome[22].

However, Hezekiah had planned carefully. In ad-

47

dition to laying up vast stores of food, Hezekiah ingeniously undertook to make available to the city under siege the life-giving waters of the Spring Gihon — a fact of which Sennacherib was apparently unaware.

In order to bring the waters of the Spring Gihon inside the city during the siege which he saw coming, Hezekiah constructed a new[23] 1750 feet tunnel, through which the Spring's waters flowed into the Pool of Siloam on the other side (the western slope) of the eastern ridge on which Jerusalem was built. Sennacherib's taunt that the Judeans would die of thirst proved in the event to be mere braggadocio; Jerusalem may well have been saved by Hezekiah's ingenious tunnel.

Hezekiah's tunnel was a remarkable engineering feat for its time and was clearly recognized as such. The biblical description is vivid:

> *When Hezekiah saw that Sennacherib intended to attack Jerusalem, he planned with his civil and military officers to stop up the water of the springs outside the city; and they helped him. They gathered together a large number of people and stopped up all the springs and the stream which flowed through the land. "Why should the kings of Assyria come here and find much water?" they asked ... Hezekiah closed the upper outlet of the waters of Gihon and directed them down to the west side of the city of David (2 Chronicles 32:2-4, 30).*

The account of Hezekiah's reign in the second book of Kings concludes:

> *The rest of the deeds of Hezekiah, his exploits and how he made the pool [Siloam] and the conduit and brought water into the city are recorded in the Book of Chronicles of the Kings of Judah (2 Kings 20:20).*

Obviously the tunnel was one of Hezekiah's major accomplishments[24].

## 7  Hezekiah's Tunnel —
## Its Features and Modern Discovery


Hezekiah's tunnel is still in existence. It still carries the waters of the Spring Gihon on the eastern slope of the City of David to the Pool of Siloam on the western slope. It can be traversed by foot, and no tourist who is able should miss the walk (Fig. 10). Directions and additional details of the tunnel are contained in the "Tour" section.

The tunnel follows an S-shaped path under the hill of Ophel, from the Spring Gihon to the Pool of Siloam. It was dug by two crews of workmen, one starting at Gihon and the other starting at what is now the Pool of Siloam. Without the assistance of any instruments which modern engineers would use — without even a magnetic compass — they managed to meet. How they managed to meet while following this serpentine path is still a mystery. But we can tell a great deal about the course of the tunneling from the evidence which the diggers left behind, much of which can be confirmed by the 20th century traveler with his own eyes.

Fig. 10. Inside Hezekiah's tunnel.

Hezekiah's northern crew first re-worked the part
of the Jebusite tunnel which Hezekiah used for his
own tunnel — and he used all he could. Hezekiah's men
cut off on their own — away from the Jebusite tunnel
— almost 65 feet after the tunnel begins, with a 90-
degree left hand turn, just before the Jebusite shaft
goes up into the mountain. You will note that in the
part of the tunnel before you make this left hand turn
the walls and ceiling show far more careful work than
the lower walls. This high quality workmanship is
probably the work of Hezekiah's men who re-worked
this part of the Jebusite tunnel; the lower walls are the

original Jebusite tunnel. The jagged path of this early part of the tunnel may have been determined by the Jebusite's search for soft rock.

Hezekiah's southern crew started afresh with a new tunnel at what is now the Pool of Siloam. The northern crew hit much harder rock than the southern crew — some of that same rock which stopped the Jebusites cold when they were forced to abandon their first shaft. As a result, the northern crew progressed more slowly than the southern crew, and the meeting point of the two crews is at a point which indicates that the southern crew dug well over 900 feet of the tunnel's 1750 feet.

Each step toward the dramatic meeting of the two crews of tunnelers can be recreated from evidence they left behind. After months and months of digging in their separate tunnels[25], wondering if they would ever meet, the tunnelers deep within the mountain heard the faint twang of the pick-axe blows of the other crew reverberating through the rock. When this happened the tunnelers were about 100 feet apart. We can tell the point at which this occurred (marked 7 and 14 on Fig. 11) because from this point on the tunneling takes on a different character. Instead of the smooth curves which characterize the tunnel's path up to this point, we now find a series of almost frenzied twists and turns, the results of the tunnelers' frantic efforts to correct their direction in response to the sound of the pick-axe blows from the crew on the other side. The first effort after the two crews heard one another was bad. Perhaps the engineers were misled by a false echo. The southern crew had the greater difficulty; they dug a three feet tunnel section before abandoning it as the wrong direction (point 13 on Fig. 11). They did the same thing 28 feet further on (point 12 on Fig. 11), when we again find a false tunnel leading from

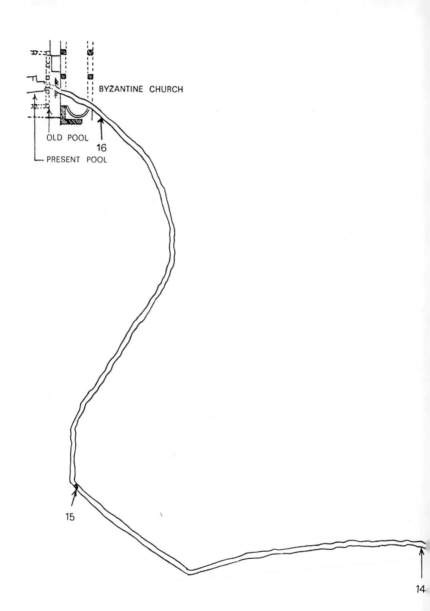

BYZANTINE CHURCH

OLD POOL

16

PRESENT POOL

15

14

Fig. 11. The plan of Hezekiah's tunnel. The following points are indicated :

(1) The beginning of the Solomonic channel which was stopped up by Hezekiah when he built his tunnel; (2) the source of the Spring Gihon; (3) the opening of a passage to the south of unknown purpose which connects with the Solomonic channel ; (4) another passage of unknown purpose; (5) the beginning of Hezekiah's tunnel; up to this point, Hezekiah re-worked the Jebusite tunnel; (6) the passage, now blocked except for a small, body-size hole, leading to the Jebusite shaft; (7) here the northern crew first heard the pick-axes of the southern crew; (8) here the northern crew first heard the voices of the southern crew; (9) the point of meeting; (10) here the southern crew first heard the voices of the northern crew; (11) the southern crew's last and shortest false tunnel; (12) the southern crew's second false tunnel; (13) the southern crew's first false tunnel; (14) here the southern crew first heard the pick-axes of the northern crew; (15) a shaft to the surface; (16) the place from which the Siloam inscription was removed.

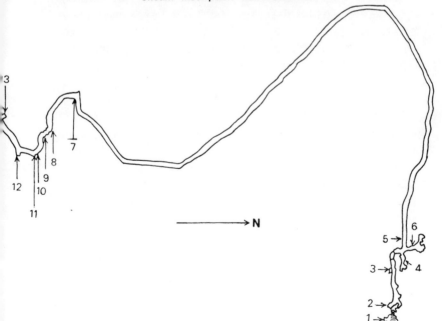

the south. The beginning of a third false tunnel is found about 13 feet further on (point 11 on Fig. 11), but by this time the southern crew is learning to correct its mistakes before it proceeds very far in the wrong direction.

The northern crew, after proceeding too directly south, corrects itself by heading southeast, and then develops a bad case of nerves, zigzagging frantically in an effort to follow the sound. First they scoop out a bit too much to the left, then too much to the right. One can almost see a workman of the northern crew with his pick-axe in hand, backing away to let the engineer examine his work with a small torch or candle. "Too far to the left" or "Too far to the right", the engineer cries. "Right in there", he says, pointing in a slightly different direction than is indicated by the little concavity that the workman intended to take. And the workman makes the correction as he raises his pick-axe to begin again, hoping soon to meet his fellow on the other side. These slight corrections can easily be seen today; it is clear that they were made by the workmen coming from the north; workmen coming from the opposite direction could not have made these scoop-outs with a forward stroke of the pick-axe. (When the corrections suddenly start facing the other direction, you know you have passed the point of meeting).

About four and a half feet apart, the workmen on one side suddenly hear not only the sound of the other crew's pick-axe blows, but also the sound of a voice calling (points 8 and 10 on Fig. 11). The call is returned and heard through the rock by the first crew. The excitement mounts. The workmen hack away feverishly, periodically calling to one another as the voices on the other side of the rock get stronger and stronger. The floor from both sides of the tunnel begins to rise.

The tunnel need not be so big, as long as they meet. (This rise in floor level is more noticeable in the southern half because it rises more sharply toward the point of juncture). And the walls of the tunnel need not be so finely finished. The almost elegant polish of the remainder of the tunnel is dispensed with as the tunnelers concentrate solely on effecting a meeting. Finally, the voices sound as if they are in the next room. A swing of the pick-axe and the point strikes through to the other side. The shouts go up. Miraculously the two sides have met. A few more blows and the workmen can see each other's faces. The two halves of the tunnel have been successfully joined.

To memorialize the great meeting, a commemorative inscription is carved in the rock wall of the tunnel near the Pool of Siloam (almost 20 feet from the Siloam entrance on the left hand side as you approach Siloam from the Spring Gihon). Written in elegant classical Hebrew, it reads as follows:

> *This is the story of the boring through. While [the tunnelers lifted] the pick-axe each toward his fellow and while 3 cubits [remained yet] to be bored [through, there was heard] the voice of a man calling his fellow — for there was a split [or overlap]²⁶ in the rock on the right hand and on [the left hand]. When the tunnel was driven through, the tunnelers hewed the rock, each man toward his fellow, pick-axe against pick-axe. And the water flowed from the spring toward the reservoir for 1200 cubits. The height of the rock above the head of the tunnelers was a hundred cubits (Fig. 12).*

Interestingly enough, the inscription does not mention the name of Hezekiah, although we would expect it to. The reason may be that the inscription was never completed. The panel on which the inscription was carved was only half used — the bottom half, consisting of six lines. Perhaps the top half was to be inscribed

Fig. 12. The Siloam Inscription in old Hebrew characters, found in Hezekiah's tunnel in 1880.

with a statement that the tunnel was the work of the great King Hezekiah in a particular year of his reign. Perhaps the Assyrian siege came sooner than expected and there was no time to complete the inscription.

This inscription was found quite by accident in June 1880 by a boy who was either playing in the tunnel near the Pool of Siloam or attempting to explore it[27]. It is inscribed in beautiful old Hebrew characters. One modern scholar has called it the "most precious of all ancient Hebrew inscriptions". It has great epigraphic significance, enabling scholars to date other Hebrew inscriptions by reference to it. Almost 100 years after its discovery, the Siloam inscription remains the longest and oldest ancient Hebrew inscription found in Israel. For rivals one must look either to the shorter, so-called Gezer calendar which may date from Solomon's time, or to the Mesha stone, a stele found on the other side of the Jordan, written in a closely related language during the second half of the 9th century B.C.E. and describing the successful rebellion of Mesha, king of Moab, against King Joram of Israel. Incidentally, the Siloam inscription also gives us some idea as to the length of the biblical cubit, probably about 18 inches.

Unfortunately, the Siloam inscription was removed from the carved rock wall by an entrepeneurial vandal shortly after it was discovered. Even before it was removed, it was cracked on its left side. But in the course of removal it broke into six or seven pieces, which soon turned up in the hands of a Greek antiquities dealer in Jerusalem. Palestine was then ruled by the Ottoman Turks, who confiscated the inscription and took it to the Museum of the Ancient Orient in Istanbul, where it still resides. However, a plaster copy may be seen at the Israel Museum in Jerusalem.

After the diggers had met, they quickly finished off the tunnel. Although they were apparently unable to take a direct path from Gihon to Siloam, they were considerably more successful in maintaining the proper level of the tunnel so far below ground — another miracle of ancient technology. Some adjustments had to be made in the tunnel floor in the southern half, which helps explain why the tunnel is as much as 18 feet high in some places near the Pool of Siloam. But with these adjustments, the tunnel floor maintains a perfectly graduated downward slope from the Spring Gihon to the Pool of Siloam, with a drop of seven feet over the course of its 1750 feet length. With this slope, the water flows evenly and steadily from the spring to the pool.

Since that part of the tunnel which passes through some of the harder rock strata of the northern half reduces to as low as five feet, the high ceiling in the southern half resulting from floor level corrections is a welcome increase in height to the traveler wading through the tunnel. If it seems a bit cramped in the short portions of the low-ceilinged area, be grateful that you are not going through with those 19th century explorers who had to crawl through the tunnel before the channel was cleared of centuries of debris and silt.

The first man in modern times to traverse the tunnel was the American orientalist Edward Robinson whose travels mark the beginning of modern archeology in Palestine (Fig. 13). Robinson crawled through the tunnel with his friend Eli Smith in 1838. Robinson first

Fig. 13. Edward Robinson, one of the great 19th century explorers of Palestine, who was the first man in modern times to go through Hezekiah's tunnel.

tried to go through from the Siloam side where the ceiling was high. However, "at the end of 800 feet, [the ceiling] became so low that we could advance no further without crawling on all fours and bringing our bodies close to the water. As we were not prepared for this, we thought it better to retreat, and try again another day from the other end". So, with the smoke from their candles, they wrote their initials and the figure 800 (feet) on the ceiling to mark where they had come and how far it was from the entrance at Siloam. Three days later they tried again, this time starting from Gihon. "Having clothed (or rather unclothed) ourselves simply in a pair of wide Arab drawers, we entered and crawled on, hoping soon to arrive at the point which we had reached from the other fountain... Most of the way we could indeed advance upon our hands and knees; yet in several places we could only get forward by lying at full length and dragging ourselves along on our elbows... At length, after having measured 950 feet, we arrived at our former mark of 800 feet traced with smoke upon the ceiling. This makes the whole length of the passage to be 1750 feet."

In 1867, Captain Charles Warren went through the tunnel, and, as we have observed, it was he who discovered the Jebusite shaft. His account too should comfort the modern traveler:

*In the month of December 1867, I made a thorough examination and survey of the passage leading from the Virgin's Fount [Gihon] to Siloam. We entered from the Siloam end, so as to have as much clean work as possible. For the first 350 feet it was plain sailing... At 450 feet the height of the passage was reduced to 3 feet 9 inches... At 600 feet it is only 2 feet 6 inches high... Our difficulties now commenced. Sergeant Birtles, with a Fellah, went ahead, measuring with tape, while I followed with compass and field-book. The bottom is a soft silt, with a calcerous crust at the top, strong enough to bear human weight, except in a few places, where it let us down with a flop... The mud silt is from 15 inches to 18 inches deep. We were now crawling on all fours, and thought we were getting on very pleasantly, the water being only 4 inches deep, and we were not wet higher than our hips. Presently bits of cabbage-stalks came floating by, and we suddenly awoke to the fact that the waters were rising. The Virgin's Fount is used as a sort of scullery to the Silwan Village, the refuse thrown there being carried off down the passage each time the water rises. The rising of the waters* had not been anticipated, as they had risen only two hours previous to our entrance. At 850 feet the height of the channel was reduced to 1 foot 10 inches, and here our troubles began. The water was running with great violence, 1 foot in height, and we, crawling full length, were up to our necks in it.

I was particularly embarrassed: one hand necessarily wet and dirty, the other holding a pencil, compass, and field-book; the candle for the most part in my mouth. Another 50 feet brought us to a place where we had regularly to run the gauntlet of the waters. The passage being only 1 foot 4 inches high, we had just 4 inches breathing space, and had some difficulty in twisting our necks round properly. When observing, my mouth was under water. At 900 feet we came upon two false cuttings, one on each side of the aqueduct. They go in for about 2 feet each... Just here I involuntarily swallowed a portion of my lead pencil for a minute or two. We were now going in a zigzag direction towards the north-west, and the height increased to 4 feet 6 inches, and at 1100 feet we were again crawling with a height of only 1 foot 10 inches. We should probably have suffered more from the cold than we did, had not our risible faculties been excited by the sight of our Fellah in front plunging and puffing through the water like a young grampus. At 1150 feet the passage again averaged in height 2 feet to 2 feet 6 inches; at 1400 feet we heard the sound of water dripping... at 1450 feet we commenced turning to the east, and the passage attained a height of 6 feet; at 1658 feet we came upon our old friend, the passage leading to the Ophel shaft, and, after a further advance of 50 feet, to the Virgin's Fount... When we came out it was dark and we had to stand shivering for some minutes before our clothes were brought us; we were nearly four hours in the water. I find a difference of 42 feet between my measurements and those of Dr. Robinson, but if he took the length of the Virgin's Fount into account, we shall very nearly agree[28].

Now the tunnel has been restored to its original condition, and the visitor can stand erect for most of the way. The average height of the tunnel is six feet. We can thank an imaginative and eccentric Finn by the name of Walter Juvelius for the fact that the tunnel has been restored. Juvelius claimed that by means of cryptography, he had extracted from the Prophet Eze-kial the location of a secret depository of biblical treasures hidden just before the Babylonian destruction of Jerusalem in 586 B.C.E. The secret hoard of trea-sures was supposed to include the original manuscript of the Law of Moses and the Ark of the Covenant. On this basis, 25,000 pounds sterling was raised among some wealthy Englishmen, who set sail in 1909 to conduct the search under the direction of a certain Captain Montague B. Parker. Neither Captain Parker nor his staff had any archeological experience or know-ledge. The Parker Mission, as it came to be called, was itself shrouded in secrecy. Armed guards kept sight-seers and scholars alike far from the site of the explo-ration — with the exception of one scholar to be noted. The public was left only to speculate. Rumors were rife. At various times during the three-year search, it was reported that the Mission had found Solomon's sword, David's crown and even the original tablets of the Law which Moses had received at Sinai. Some said these treasures had been secreted out of the country.

The search was in fact concentrated on the Spring Gihon and the surrounding area. It continued for three years without success. However, the Parker Mission did thoroughly explore the tunnel system under the hill of Ophel and restore it to its present condition. In addition, the Mission agreed to allow Père L.H. Vincent of the Ecole Biblique et Archéologique Française to follow its course, and measure and record the explora-tions. As a result, the mission was fruitful scientifically, if not cryptographically[29]. Père Vincent's writings are the most authorative descriptions of the underground water systems on the hill of Ophel. However, the sage Dominican scholar says not a word about the identity of the sponsors of the Mission, nor what their aim was.

When the search of the Gihon area proved fruitless, the Parker Mission secretly and without permission of the Turkish authorities began digging at night under the sacred Temple Mount, in the area known popularly as Solomon's stables and in certain tunnels north of the Temple area. To gain access to the Temple compound at night, the Englishmen dressed in fezzes and Arab dress. In this manner, and by bribing some officials, they were able to dig for nine nights without detection. However, the excavation was then discovered by the Turkish authorities and promptly stopped. Word of the digging in this area — sacred to Moslems as well as Jews — spread through the city like wildfire. It was the time of an annual Moslem pilgrimage to Jerusalem, and thousands of religious Moslems crowded the city. When word of the unlawful excavations in the holy area broke, anti-Christian riots were threatened and were barely averted. The Englishmen fled to their yacht anchored off Jaffa, and secretly departed the land. Although the Turkish Governor of Jerusalem had not approved the digging in the sacred area under the Temple Mount, he was nevertheless dismissed from his post. And that was the end of the Parker Mission — except for Père Vincent's valuable publications.

# 8 Remaining Questions and Some New Answers

When Kathleen Kenyon finished her excavations on the hill of Ophel in 1967, she found that she had not only answered a number of long-standing and difficult questions in the archeology of Jerusalem, but she had also raised some new ones. One of the most difficult of these new questions concerned the outlet to Hezekiah's tunnel at the Pool of Siloam.

The 1961-67 excavations in the area of the Pool established with a very high degree of probability the location of the western wall of the City of David on the other side of the ridge from the Spring Gihon. However, Miss Kenyon placed the western wall of David's city higher up on the ridge than the Pool of Siloam. In other words, the Pool of Siloam was outside the city wall, and Hezekiah's tunnel directed the waters of the Spring Gihon from one point outside the city walls *to another point outside the city walls !*

Did Miss Kenyon make a mistake in locating the city's western wall? Although she conceded that her location of the western wall of the City of David was based on "negative" evidence — she did not find the wall itself — still, her argument carries a great deal of logical persuasion as well as expert authority. Yet why would Hezekiah leave the outlet to his tunnel exposed outside the city wall?

Miss Kenyon struggled manfully — or should we say womanfully — with the apparent fact that the Pool of Siloam was outside the city walls, and came up with an answer which to her was "completely satisfactory". Miss Kenyon conjectured that what we know as the Pool of Siloam was itself a concealed rock-cut cistern which could be entered by another stairs and shaft from within the town wall.

However, Miss Kenyon has not been able to find any trace of the cistern which she suspects was probably at the Pool of Siloam, nor has she found any trace of any entry to it from within the wall of the city. There is, however, a long-exposed rock channel for the overflow of water from the Pool of Siloam; Miss Kenyon argues that this channel, which leads to the central valley where the Kidron and Hinnom Valleys join, was used to conceal the source of the overflow water as coming from the cistern at the Pool of Siloam.

On the other hand, why would Hezekiah start the western end of the tunnel *outside* the city wall. After all, he chose in advance the spot where the tunnel was to emerge. It was from the spot which *he chose* that the second crew of tunnelers dug in the direction of the Spring Gihon. Moreover, the Bible tells us that Hezekiah brought the water "into the city".

It is a mark of the speed with which the archeological world now moves that we can record a new answer to the problem. In 1970, Professor N. Avigad of the Hebrew University reported the results of his recent excavations in the Jewish Quarter of the Old City of Jerusalem. At a site about 900 feet west of the Western Wall of the Temple Mount (the so-called Wailing Wall), Professor Avigad found a massive fortification wall over 20 feet thick (Fig. 14). He dates this wall from about the time of King Hezekiah and suggests

Fig. 14. The fortification wall uncovered in the Old City in 1970 by Professor N. Avigad, who believes this was part of the outer wall which enclosed the Pool of Siloam in Hezekiah's time.

that he is the most likely builder of the wall. This ascription is supported by the biblical text which credits Hezekiah with building "another wall without" (2 Chronicles 32:5), that is, a second wall outside the original city wall[30].

Professor Avigad was able to expose about 130 feet of the newly-discovered wall, which contained two angles. From this the wall can be extrapolated in two directions. Taking into account the topography of the land and other archeological remains, Professor Avigad has been able to conjecture as to the remaining course of the new fortification wall. The result of this conjecture is shown on Fig. 15[30a]. As you will see, this new wall encloses the Pool of Siloam and solves the problem of Hezekiah's bringing the waters of Gihon "into the city"[31]. (Unfortunately, the excavated portion of this newly-discovered wall cannot now be seen, since construction is going on around it. However, the buildings have been designed to leave the wall exposed and visitors will be able to see it once again when the buildings have been completed. The wall is located just northwest of the remains of the Nissan Bek Synagogue).

In fairness to Miss Kenyon, it should be said that she considered the possibility of such a second wall enlarging the city. But she rejected it on the ground that any such wall would have to be in "a position quite unacceptable on military grounds". Thus is scholarly theorizing contradicted by fact. Or perhaps we should say that thus is scholarly theorizing contradicted by scholarly conjecture. At any rate, that is where the solution to the problem now stands.

A final mystery about Hezekiah's tunnel remains. Why does it follow such a serpentine course? As a result of these curves, the length of the tunnel is increased by more than a third. There is no satisfactory

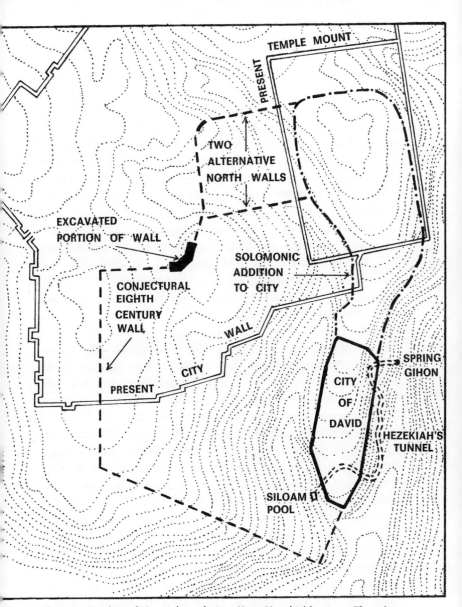

Fig. 15. A plan of Jerusalem during King Hezekiah's time. The plan
also shows the first expansion of the city northward during King
Solomon's time to accommodate his new palace and the Temple. Note
the newly-excavated fortification wall dating from King Hezekiah's
time and Professor Avigad's suggestion as to the remaining course
of this wall. The two northern walls are alternative suggestions.

answer to this question — not even a reasonably satisfactory one. It has been suggested that the S-curve of the tunnel was the result of the tunnelers search for soft rock. But if this were true, we would expect false starts, hesitations and wavering progress instead of the sure, steady curves we find in both the northern and southern loop of the S. Moreover, the suggestion that the tunnelers were searching for soft rock is contradicted by the geological facts[32].

The argument of "technical inability" as put forth by some scholars is equally groundless, as proven by the tunnel systems both at Megiddo and at Gezer. Indeed as far as technical ability is concerned, it is technically more difficult to connect up two curved tunnels — which Hezekiah's tunnelers did — than two straight tunnels.

In the absence of any better explanation, some scholars have suggested that the tunnelers simply made a mistake. However, it would be easy enough for the tunnelers to know when they ceased following a straight line because their light would be cut off.

The most intriguing suggestion, put forward at the end of the last century by the French scholar Clermont-Ganneau, is that the southern curve of the tunnel was taken to avoid the royal tombs of the kings of Judah[33]. It must be conceded the theory has a certain charm. The Bible records that David and the 12 Judean kings following him were buried within the "City of David". The usual formula is "He was buried with his fathers in the City of David" (e.g., 1 Kings 11:43; 15:24; 22:51). Although the common people were buried outside the city, the Bible is clear that that was not the case with regard to the kings. Based on the description of the city walls in the third chapter of *Nehemiah* — which also contains a reference to the burial place of David — some scholars were able, they thought, to locate the royal necropolis in the southern part of the city, close to the eastern wall — within the southern loop of Hezekiah's tunnel. In 1913 and again in 1923, expeditions headed by the French archeologist Raymond Weill were organized to test this theory and hopefully to find the royal tombs. Clermont-Ganneau had predicted they would find not only the tombs, but also royal treasure to rival the Pharoahs of Egypt. Several sets of tombs were in fact found within the southern loop of Hezekiah's tunnel (Fig. 26). Unfortunately, they had been robbed not only of any treasures they may have contained, but of archeological contents as well. However, the tombs themselves do appear to be more than the sepulchres of ordinary people. One especially can be visualized close to its original form, with a place for the sarcophagus clearly marked; it would have been an impressive tomb, easily suggesting royal contents (Figs 16 and 17).

On the available evidence, it is impossible to say with any degree of certainty whether or not Weill has found the royal necropolis of the kings of Judah. It is tempting to think he has, although many scholars believe the tombs are later. But even if he has found the royal necropolis, this probably does not explain the shape of Hezekiah's tunnel. At best, it would explain the southern loop, not the northern loop. And half an explanation is hardly better than none. Moreover, Weill's necropolis could have been avoided just as surely and far more easily by a straight tunnel from Siloam to Gihon. Then the tunnel would have passed to the west of the necropolis. Some explanation needs to be given why instead Hezekiah decided to enclose the alleged royal necropolis by a curve on three sides. Finally, Weill found another set of tombs south of the southern loop of Hezekiah's tunnel. Thus the loop of the tunnel did not go around all of the tombs he exca-

Fig. 16. The largest and most magnificent of the tombs in the necropolis. There is a depression at the end of the tunnel for a 4-feet wide sarcophagus. The hole in the lower center part of the picture may be the entrance to a tomb dug at a later date under the larger tomb, when the cemetery became crowded. At that time, it is thought that an artificial floor was placed at the floor level of the larger tomb. The crevice in the rock into which the new floor support was fitted can be plainly seen.

vated, only the first ones. This led Weill himself to reject Clermont-Ganneau's explanation of the southern loop. But other archeologists contend that this southernmost set of tombs is different from the others — not so grand — and does not of itself contradict Clermont-Ganneau's theory. Still others argue that even if the royal tombs were confined to the interior of the southern loop, this offers no explanation for the loop.

Fig. 17.  The view looking out from the large tomb described in the
previous picture.

The tunnel goes far below the tombs and the tunnelers
would not be concerned, so this argument runs, at digging beneath the royal tombs. All of the arguments,
pro and con, regarding the southern loop can be sum-
marized as "not proven"[34]. Whether we will ever be

able to speak with greater certainty about the royal tombs of the kings of Judah, no one can say.

Above the Pool of Siloam is a mosque. The site was originally a Byzantine church. Shortly after the church was excavated at the end of the last century, a mosque was built over it in response to a supposed command of Mohammed given to a Silwan villager in a vision. Thus almost no remains of the church can be seen.

To the south of the pool is a well-watered garden served by the flow from the pool. In the area of this garden was the original Pool of Siloam, which, with adjacent gardens, was probably constructed by King Solomon[35]. Remains of a pre-Hezekiah channel have been found which carried the waters of Gihon directly south from the spring to this pool and garden area (see Fig. 18). The entrance and outlets to this channel can still be seen (see "Tour Section" for exact directions). On the way, this channel irrigated the cultivated terraces of the eastern slope of the ridge through a number of smaller apertures. Because this channel and the apertures were for the most part visible and unprotected, scholars conjecture that the channel was built in a time of peace and security. Solomon's reign was of course one of great political tranquility, the only one in the early monarchy, so the attribution to Solomon seems quite probable. Although *Ecclesiastes* was written much later, it speaks in the name of King Solomon and recalls his works: "I made myself gardens and parks and planted all kinds of fruit-trees in them. I made myself pools of water to irrigate a grove of growing trees" (Ecclesiastes 2:4-5). The reference may be to this channel and the adjacent gardens, the remains of which can still be seen, as can the lush green foliage nourished by the same waters.

Hezekiah stopped up this channel when he built

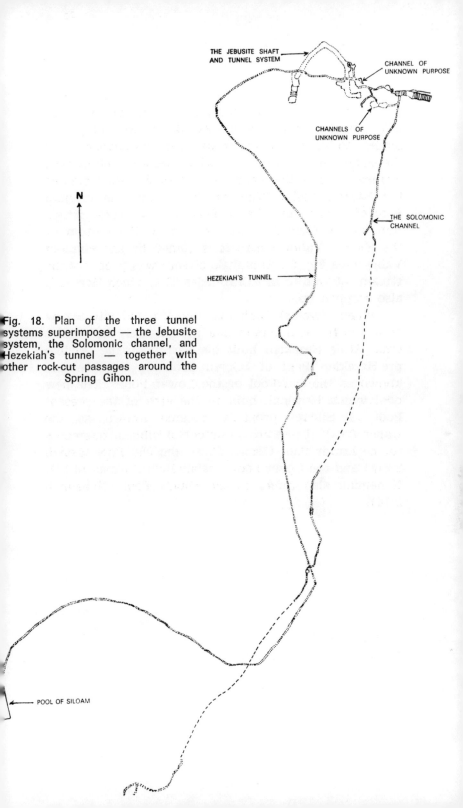

THE JEBUSITE SHAFT
AND TUNNEL SYSTEM

CHANNEL OF
UNKNOWN PURPOSE

CHANNELS OF
UNKNOWN PURPOSE

N

THE SOLOMONIC
CHANNEL

HEZEKIAH'S TUNNEL

Fig. 18. Plan of the three tunnel systems superimposed — the Jebusite system, the Solomonic channel, and Hezekiah's tunnel — together with other rock-cut passages around the Spring Gihon.

POOL OF SILOAM

his tunnel to the other side of the city, and the biblical reference to Hezekiah's stopping up the springs outside the city (2 Chronicles 32:3-4) is probably a reference to his closing off these irrigation channels and the small outlets from them which watered the eastern terraces outside the walls, as well as the other side of the Kidron Valley. The overflow from the original Pool of Siloam and the rivulets from all these irrigation outlets formed a little stream at the bottom of the Kidron Valley where it is joined by the Hinnom Valley (see Fig. 2). This little stream was probably the stream referred to in 2 Chronicles 32:4, which Hezekiah also stopped up.

When Hezekiah built his tunnel, it fed into a new pool, which was no doubt much larger than the present tank. After Hezekiah built his new pool, the original pre-Hezekiah Pool of Siloam probably then became known as the Old Pool or the Lower Pool[36]. The new pool which Hezekiah built in the area of the present Pool of Siloam probably became known as the Upper Pool[37]. There are a number of biblical references to the Lower Pool (Isaiah 22:9), the Old Pool (Isaiah 22:11) and the Upper Pool (Isaiah 36:2; 2 Kings 18:17); Nehemiah also refers to the King's Pool (Nehemiah 2:14).

# 9 Gihon and Siloam in Later History

The Pool of Siloam was apparently in a fashionable part of town when Jerusalem was rebuilt during the time of Ezra and Nehemiah. Nehemiah records that the walls of the Pool of Siloam were rebuilt by one Shallun; it was located next to the King's Garden (Nehemiah 3:15). That the pool continued to be a lovely watering spot can be seen from the reconstruction of the city during the time of Herod the Great (37-4 B.C.E.) at the Holyland West Hotel. There the pool is pictured in an elegant Hellenistic setting.

For Jesus, the waters of Siloam apparently had special healing power. As recorded in John 9:1-12, Jesus cured a blind man by making a paste of earth and spittle which he placed on the blind man's eyes with instructions to wash off the paste in the waters of Siloam. When he did so, the blind man was able to see.

In Christian times, the Spring Gihon was often referred to as the Virgin's Fount[38], for here, legend has it, the Virgin washed the infant Jesus' clothes. Today Arab women can still be seen in the morning washing clothes and even rugs in the Pool of Siloam[39] (see Fig. 25).

Both the Spring Gihon and the Pool of Siloam, as well as the excavations in the City of David could be more attractively presented to the visitor today. But that will perhaps come in time. In the meantime, with a little imagination, it is still possible to appreciate these remains of ancient Jerusalem if one understands them. There is no other place in the Holy City where one can come as close to the world of the Hebrew Bible as here in the original City of David.

# The Tour

## 1 The Spring Gihon

The Spring Gihon can be reached easily from Jerusalem by bus, private car or taxi. Take bus number 76 from the East Jerusalem Central Bus Station opposite the Damascus Gate and get off at the Spring Gihon. By car, take the Jericho Road and make a right turn, going down into the Kidron Valley, at Siloah Street. Absalom's Tomb will be seen immediately on the left, followed by some other large Hellenistic tombs (you must look backward to see the latter). None dates from the biblical period and all attributions to the contrary are traditional, not factual. The entrance to the Spring Gihon can be seen on the right, inside a chain-link fence that is used as a playground by an adjacent school. (The school is the first building you reach on your right.)

The entrance to the spring is by two levels of stairs, which are medieval structures. From the top of

Fig. 19. Looking out and up the steps from the cave in which the Spring Gihon is located. Part of the natural cave can be seen at the lower left. During time of danger and siege, the entrance to the cave was blocked up and camouflaged.

the second set of stairs, you can see that you are entering a natural cave, in which the spring gushes forth (Fig. 19). This water supply determined the site to be chosen for the original city of Jerusalem (see section on "Background", p. 19).

After looking at the spring, and before entering the tunnel, come back up the stairs to examine the mountain above.

## 2 The Jebusite Wall

On the right of the Spring Gihon (and on the right of a refreshment stand beside the spring) is a long set of stairs. Go up these stairs about 150 feet (77 stairs). You will see a path to the excavations on your right. Follow this path a mere 25 feet and you will be standing in front of the Jebusite and Davidic wall of Jerusalem, the only section which remains exposed (see Fig. 20). Walk up the steps on the path and you will see the wall from the direction pictured in Fig. 3. The angle in the wall initially suggested to the excavator either that the wall had a series of insets or that she had hit a gate tower. When later excavations revealed a further section of the wall to the north that ran into the side of the angle (rather than meeting it), she concluded the angle was part of a gate tower, probably the main gate used to get to the Spring Gihon during time of peace. The wall was originally built by the Jebusites in about 1800 B.C.E. It was repaired by King David and used continuously thereafter by the Israelites until about 750 B.C.E.

This wall was then succeeded by another wall, all trace of which has disapppeared. The wall directly behind the Jebusite wall dates from the 8th century, B.C.E., and was used until the Babylonian destruction in 586 B.C.E. It shows many reconstructions and repairs (see Figs. 3 and 20). The walls immediately above and behind this one are modern terracing.

When the wall of Jerusalem was rebuilt by Nehemiah after the Babylonian exile (about 445 B.C.E.), he abandoned the steep eastern slope and constructed his east wall of the city higher on the crest of the ridge, as we shall see at a later point on our tour (see Fig. 20).

←

Fig. 20. View of the northern part of the hill of Ophel. The south wall of the present old city is in the background. The two-windowed building at the bottom of the picture sits over the Spring Gihon. Going up the steps, the first wall directly behind the house in the lower center part of the picture is the Jebusite wall built about 1800 B.C.E. The wall directly behind it was built and used by the Israelites from about 750 B.C.E. to the Babylonian destruction of Jerusalem in 586 B.C.E. The series of walls behind this are modern terracing walls. At a level of the fourth modern terrace wall is the point where the Jebusite watershaft came out within the Jebusite city. On the crest of the hill can be seen the line of structures previously thought to be the Jebusite defense line, now known to be a line established by Nehemiah when he returned from the Babylonian exile. Following this line from left to right, we see a Maccabean tower formerly thought to have been built by David; a later supporting step-like construction (part of which was removed in the 1961—1967 excavations; the part that was removed is in the shadow cast by the large tower; the part that remains is to the right of the shadow); a smaller post-exilic tower; and, to the right of this tower, some of the original wall built by Nehemiah.

# 3 The Top of the Jebusite Shaft

Coming back to the modern concrete stairs, continue up the stairs another 80 feet, or 44 stairs, and you will see a path on your left and a few steps leading down and backward toward the path on which you stand. Take these few steps down and walk about 40 feet until you see a tunnel on your left (Fig. 21) leading to the opening of the Jebusite shaft which is now unfortunately filled up and inaccessible. A few feet to the northwest of this visible tunnel opening is the beginning of the tunnel system through which the Jebusites brought the waters of Gihon into the city during time of war, danger and siege (see section on "Background", pp. 27-30). Note that you are higher up on the ridge of Ophel than the Jebusite wall, and are therefore inside the city.

With modern equipment, it would not be difficult to open the Jebusite shaft and tunnel system from within the original city wall. After all, the Parker Mission did it 60 years ago. With a few electrical lights and a railing, visitors would once again be able to examine this ancient water system which is freighted with so much historical significance. Only the lack of public interest stands in the way of the project's being carried out.

Fig. 21. A little-known tunnel leading to the blocked-up entrance to the Jebusite shaft and tunnel system within the Jebusite city wall. The tunnel is probably the work of the Parker Mission.

# 4 The So-Called Tower of David, Nehemiah's Wall and 7th Century B.C.E. Israelite Homes Destroyed in the Babylonian Destruction

Returning to the concrete steps, continue the walk up to the back of a modern house and the top of the hill. Now follow the steps to the right (north) for 90 feet (30 steps). Ahead of you, you will see a massive revetment of stones about 50 feet from the main path (see Fig. 22). Take the path down to get a full frontal view. This mass of stones are the remains of a tower excavated by R.A.S. Macalister during his excavations on the hill of Ophel between 1923 and 1925. The tower

➜

Fig. 22. Macalister's so-called "Tower of David". Note the figure at base of tower which gives some idea of the size of the tower. The four upper courses of masonry are different from those below. These four upper courses were mistakenly attributed by Macalister to King Solomon, the remainder of the tower to King David. Until the 1961—1967 excavations, the Jebusite wall and defenses were thought to be in a line with this tower. In fact, this line, higher up on the ridge, is the line established by Nehemiah in about 445 B.C.E., when he abandoned as part of the city the destroyed lower slopes. The tower is in fact a Maccabean addition to Nehemiah's wall.

was part of a wall circumvallating the ridge (see Fig. 20). Macalister confirmed (wrongfully, of course) previous identifications of this wall as the original Jebusite defenses of the city, and assigned all but the top four courses of the tower itself to King David's time. The tower promptly became dubbed the "Tower of David"[40].

To the right (north) of the large tower is a rough, glacis-like or step-like construction seemingly supporting the wall. This was identified by Macalister — again incorrectly — as a Jebusite rampart or bastion. Further to the right is a smaller tower[41].

When Miss Kenyon began her excavations in the summer of 1961, she was troubled by the fact that the

alleged Jebusite and Davidic defenses of the city were so high up on the ridge — higher than the outlet to the Jebusite watershaft. The Jebusite watershaft was supposed to bring the waters of Gihon inside the city. Yet Macalister's so-called Tower of David and Jebusite bastion were higher up on the ridge than the outlet to the Jebusite watershaft. Therefore, reasoned Miss Kenyon, the real Jebusite wall must lie undiscovered at a point on the ridge below the outlet to the Jebusite watershaft. For that reason, Miss Kenyon dug her first trench in 1961 south from Macalister's tower and there she found the Jebusite wall dating from about 1800 B.C.E., at a point lower on the ridge than the outlet to the Jebusite watershaft, thus placing this watershaft outlet inside the Jebusite city.

Miss Kenyon also excavated beneath and adjacent to Macalister's tower. At a level beneath the tower, she found the ruins of 7th century B.C.E. Israelite houses which had been destroyed in the Babylonian destruction of Jerusalem in 586 B.C.E. Obviously a Davidic tower (c. 1000 B.C.E.) could not have been built on top of 7th century houses.

The remains of these Israelite houses can still be seen at the base of Macalister's large tower[42]. The best preserved are those just north (to the right) of Macalister's large tower where two monolithic stone columns which supported the roof may still be seen. A few steps leading to an upper terrace have also been preserved (Fig. 23). These Israelite houses are the only rooms which can still be seen in Jerusalem which date from Old Testament times. The walls of these houses are made of roughly-shaped stones which were probably originally covered with mud-plaster. But they do not come from a period of great prosperity and they do not reflect a high level of workmanship.

When Nehemiah rebuilt the wall of Jerusalem after

his return from the Babylonian exile, he followed the line of the old city wall, except on this eastern side of the city. There the terraces on the eastern slope had been destroyed and a rebuild of the wall on this steep rubble would have been laborious and time-consuming. Moreover, Nehemiah did not need the additional space anyway. Fewer people inhabited the city in Nehemiah's time than before the Babylonian destruction. A wall on the top of the crest also made sense from a military point of view. Therefore, Nehemiah abandoned the eastern slope of the ridge and built his wall higher

Fig. 23. At a level beneath the tower in the previous picture, archeologists in the 1960's found the remains of some 7th century B.C.E. Israelite houses destroyed in the Babylonian destruction of Jerusalem in 586 B.C.E. This picture shows some steps leading to a second floor terrace (on the left), a monolithic column to support the roof (on the right) and a house wall (in the center).

up — on the comparatively level crest of the hill. This is confirmed by the biblical record as well as by the archeological evidence: The biblical description of the rebuilding of the walls uses the names of the gates of the city as landmarks, except for a portion which is described by other markers including private homes. This part of the biblical description using private homes probably refers to the new eastern wall when the original wall lower down the slope was abandoned (Nehemiah 3). Some of the original wall of Nehemiah can be seen to the right (north) of the small tower, north of Macalister's so-called Jebusite bastion (Fig. 20).

Macalister's Tower of David turned out to be a Maccabean structure of the second half of the 2d century B.C.E., for the purpose of strengthening the city's fortifications at that point. The so-called Jebusite bastion is even later[43]. Macalister died, an old man, in 1951, so he never learned that his Tower of David was in fact built about 850 years after David's reign.

# 5 The Underground Tunnel Systems — From the Time of the Jebusites, King Solomon and King Hezekiah

Return to the Spring Gihon and prepare to enter the water. The trip through the tunnel takes about 20 or 30 minutes, and is best done in tennis shoes and shorts or swimming trunks. The water level varies depending on the time of day and year, but it rarely rises above waist level. There are usually a few young Arabs at the entrance to the tunnel at the Spring Gihon who will lead you through with a handful of small candles, or, more recently, with a flashlight. However, it is a good idea to bring your own flashlight to examine the details of this remarkable tunnel.

On the way down the steps, stop at the tenth step of the second set of steps (counting from the landing after the first set of steps). Look to your left and you will see a channel leading to the south (see Fig. 18, p. 73). This is the beginning of Solomon's irrigation channel, through which the waters of Gihon flowed to irrigate the terraces on the eastern slope of the ridge and the garden at the southern end of Ophel. When Hezekiah built his tunnel, this channel was stopped up and no longer used.

The first 65 feet of Hezekiah's tunnel follows the course of the original Jebusite tunnel. The ceiling and upper walls have been reworked by Hezekiah's workmen. The lower walls are Jebusite. (Originally Hezekiah raised the floor of the original Jebusite channel to send the waterflow into his own channel. In the course of clearing the tunnel, the excavators removed this fill). The path of these first 65 feet is jagged and passes through some natural caves. Shortly after passing through these natural caves, you will see on your left, just above the water line, a channel leading south (see Fig. 18). The purpose of this channel is not known. It connects with another channel of unknown purpose, and it also leads to the Solomonic channel, noted above (see Fig. 18), which led from the Spring Gihon directly south for irrigation purposes — until Hezekiah stopped it up.

Beyond the entry to this channel of unknown purpose, the tunnel takes a right hand turn and, about 15 feet further on, a sharp 90-degree left hand turn. This sharp left hand turn marks the beginning of Hezekiah's own tunneling. But stop before entering. Take time to notice that there is also a dead-end channel on your right (see Fig. 18). Look inside with your flashlight. It is all visible from this point. This dead-end channel may have been an early Jebusite attempt to raise a shaft. Or, if you wish to speculate, it could once have been a secret depository for sacred objects or other treasure. No one knows what its purpose was.

Now, before turning left into the new part of the tunnel constructed by Hezekiah's workmen, look straight ahead. There is a small hole in the wall, large enough, however, to admit a man's body. (The writer has climbed through with the help of two trusted Arab

Fig. 24. A rare picture looking up a Jebusite shaft, taken during the Parker Mission, 1909—1911. See also Fig. 7.

companions, so he can attest it can be done). Put your flashlight into this hole. You are now looking at the base of the Jebusite shaft through which David may have captured the Jebusite city of Jerusalem (see section on "Background", pp. 34-37). If you were able to enter this enclosure (which is not recommended), you would be able to look up into this jagged, rocky shaft (see Figs. 11 and 24). It is a moving sight.

Now make the left hand turn into Hezekiah's tunnel (see Fig. 11). The walls and ceiling are well-shaped and carefully chipped. The path is gently curving or straight. You will be able to walk quickly and comfortably. Generally you will be able to stand upright. But the rock in this northern part of the tunnel is hard and sometimes the height of the tunnel goes down to as low as five feet or a bit less. However, these low passages are not long.

Soon you find yourself in a series of short curves, back and forth. When this happens you will know that you have reached the point where the two crews of tunnelers heard one another and began to attempt to effect a joinder by following the sound. Just before some of these turns, you will notice a small scooped-out section where the tunneler was apparently going to dig until corrected by his superior. It is easy to see that these scoops could only have been made by a tunneler coming from the north; a tunneler working from the other direction could not turn his pick-axe round to make these scoops. You will also notice the floor gently rising because the tunnelers failed to maintain the floor level in their excited effort to effect a joinder. The chips and finish on the walls and ceiling become rougher and less polished as the tunnelers single-mindedly seek the other half of the channel.

Suddenly you will notice that the scoop-outs are facing the other direction. You have just passed the point of juncture. You may want to go back to examine the marks from the pick-axe blows to see if you can find the point of juncture.

From the point of juncture onward, all the false starts are in the other direction. They were made by the crew coming from the south. There are three false channels near the point of juncture in the southern half, although the first one (coming from the north) is so short you may not count it. The mistake here was corrected quickly. But the other two are easily noticeable and you may actually walk in them.

Next you will come to a long, straight portion of the tunnel, easily transversed. In the southern half of the channel where the rock is soft and less compact, there are also several naturally eroded caves, ledges, faults and holes, both on the walls and ceiling. Two large holes in the ceiling are especially noticeable. At one time they were both identified as shafts to the surface. Actually only one of them, the second, is a shaft to the surface, and even it is now filled with large boulders. It is especially important to call attention to this shaft, because it is frequently and incorrectly pointed out to the unsuspecting tourist as the "shaft of David". Obviously, the shaft of David could not lead into the southern part of Hezekiah's subsequently-dug tunnel. This shaft reaches ground level at the point in the course of the tunnel where the distance between the tunnel and the ground level is shortest. The shaft was perhaps dug as an air-hole for the southern crew of tunnelers. If so, it could in part account for the faster progress made by the southern crew. Or the shaft could have been dug later by an enterprising Israelite who wanted his own private well. In any event, it is not David's shaft.

Further along are two panels on the right hand wall, incised about one half inch. One of these can be located just inside the first of two modern iron bar-gates which cross the tunnel near the Pool of Siloam. This is often pointed out — incorrectly — as the place from which the Siloam inscription was removed. Obviously an inscription carved on the wall could not have been removed in 1880 by such a shallow and neatly squared-off impression — especially by amateur vandals. This fact will become even clearer when you examine the true cavity left by the vandals who did take the inscription. The panels which are wrongly pointed out as the places from which the inscription was removed appear to be the beginning of the preparation of a part of the wall so that it could be inscribed. However, not even the preparation of the panels was completed, and the inscriptions were never made. More we do not know.

About 20 feet before you come out at the Pool of Siloam you will find in the left hand wall, just above the water line, the hole which was actually made by the vandals who removed the Siloam inscription. Opposite this point, on the opposite wall, is a triangular hole in which, it has been suggested, the workman carving the inscription inserted his torch. Other triangular niches appear irregularly throughout the tunnel and may have served the same purpose. Or perhaps more likely, a peg was placed in the hole, secured by a couple of stones, and a light hung on the peg.

# 6  The Pool of Siloam and The Mosque

A few steps further and you are in the tank which is now the Pool of Siloam. For centuries, going as far back as Josephus, it was thought that Siloam was a spring, the connection between Gihon and Siloam having been forgotten. Until the last century, Siloam was known as the Fountain of Siloam rather than the Pool of Siloam. (See Fig. 25 for a view of the Pool of Siloam as it existed in the 19th century.)

Note the mosque above the Pool of Siloam. It was originally the site of a Byzantine church that was excavated by Bliss and Dickie. The only part of this church that can still be seen is a small piece of Byzantine wall and cornice. From the top of the steps leading down to the Pool, the wall is visible to the right of the Mosque and is painted yellow. The column bases in the Pool may be from the Byzantine church, but they are not *in situ*.

Fig. 25. The Pool of Siloam as shown in a 19th century engraving.

# 7 The King's Garden, the Old Pool, The Rock-Cut Scarp and Solomon's Irrigation Channel

After climbing up the steps of the Pool of Siloam, turn left. Walk down toward the Kidron Valley road. On your right you will see a well-watered garden. In this area was the original Pool of Siloam, probably built by King Solomon and served by water brought from Gihon by a channel leading directly south from Gihon along the eastern slope (see Fig. 18). Adjacent to the pool was the King's Garden.

On your left you will see a rock cut channel at the base of the scarp which still carries overflow water from the Pool of Siloam. This channel was once covered; that is, it was originally a tunnel. Someone in ancient times — we don't know who — cut away the southern point of the hill of Ophel and exposed the channel, leaving the scarp as it is seen today. Nor do we know why this point of the hill was removed — perhaps to secure the city's southern defenses or perhaps the result of a quarrying operation. The channel was probably used in Hezekiah's time, as it is today, to carry away the overflow from the Pool of Siloam — except that in Hezekiah's day the channel was an underground tunnel.

Shortly after the point where the water flows underground again, you will see a hole or small tunnel in the rock on your left. This is the exit of the Solomonic irrigation channel[44], the beginning of which we saw on the steps going down to the Spring Gihon. Proceed to the road. Follow the scarp around the corner (going north) and just before the little antiquities shop you will see another larger tunnel in the rock, with an iron gate. This is where the curving Solomonic irrigation channel, which flowed for some of its course outside, re-entered the rock as a tunnel[45]. The tunnel can be explored for about 40 feet and is worth a visit[46].

Now cross the street and look over the ledge on the other side of the road to see the flow from the Spring Gihon proceeding into the valley and watering acres of lush vegetation which was once part of the King's Garden.

# 8  The Tombs Attributed to the Kings of Judah, The Stairway of David, The Synagogue Inscription, And the Tower of Siloam

Re-cross the street and proceed five steps upward toward the Pool of Siloam. On your right (going north) is a path. Take this path up the hill.

You begin by going up the remains of some steps carved into the rock. The Bible makes several references to stairs going up to or down from the City of David (Nehemiah 3:15; 12:37). In the opinion of many scholars, the upper part of these steps are the remains of the stairway referred to in Nehemiah. The steps are commonly called the stairway of David*.

---

* About this stairway one eminent scholar has written:
  This staircase, though badly damaged in its lower section, will always rank as one of the most precious archeological 'illustrations' of the Old Testament ever discovered in Palestine. It is an almost heart-breaking fact that the municipality of Jerusalem completely fails to protect an historic monument of such a quality from further gradual demolition and annihilation. [J. Simons, Review, Bibliotheca Orientalis, Vol. VI, p. 20 (1949)].
Nothing has changed in this regard since 1949.

Fig. 26. A general view of the necropolis (within the southern loop of Hezekiah's tunnel) thought by many scholars to be the royal tombs of the kings of Judah. The entrances to two impressive tunnel tombs can be seen in the upper part of the picture. What appears to be rock terracing is in fact the result of a Roman quarrying operation to obtain masonry to build Aelia Capitolina in 135 C.E.

Proceeding up the hill you will see a Moslem grave on your left. On your right, you will see the remains of a large ancient cistern and some excavations about which we shall comment on the return walk. Continue on the path up the hill past these excavations to a much larger site of excavations which are again on your right. Take the path on your right on the rim of the excavations and follow it around the small hill,

which is an archeologist's dump. This site can be recognized from the picture in Fig. 26. The site is cha-
racterized by two prominent features: by a series of
what appear to be terraces carved in the rock, and by
two short passageways or tunnels also carved into the
rock. The rock terraces are in fact the remains of a
Roman quarrying operation. The large squared-off holes
in the ground are also quarries. From these quarries
the Romans obtained masonry to build Aelia Capitolina in 135 C.E., at which time the original City of David
was not included in the city. This in part explains why
so little of the original structures on the hill of Ophel
can be found: the stones were taken to build Aelia
Capitolina. What remains of this particular quarry
looks as if it could have been designed by a modern
landscape architect.

The two outstanding rock-cut passages or tunnels
are in fact tombs uncovered by Weill in his 1913-1914
excavations. (A path behind the hill leads down into
the quarry and tomb area.) The longer passage is an
especially impressive tomb (see Figs. 16 and 17). Two
and a half feet before the end of the tunnel is a depression or cavity in the floor where the sarcophagus
was probably placed (see Fig. 27). From the size of the
depression — four feet wide — it is obvious that the
sarcophagus must have been both large and magnificent
— perhaps belonging to one of the early kings of Judah,
possibly even David or Solomon. No more likely candi-
date for the tomb of these kings has been uncovered.

The holes in the rock in the front of this large
tomb are thought to be entrances to tombs at a lower
level (see Figs. 16 and 27). As the royal cemetery became
crowded, more space was obtained by digging lower
level tombs beneath the earlier tombs. On both sides
of the entrance to the large tomb, you will see a groove
which, it is conjectured, was to hold an arched floor

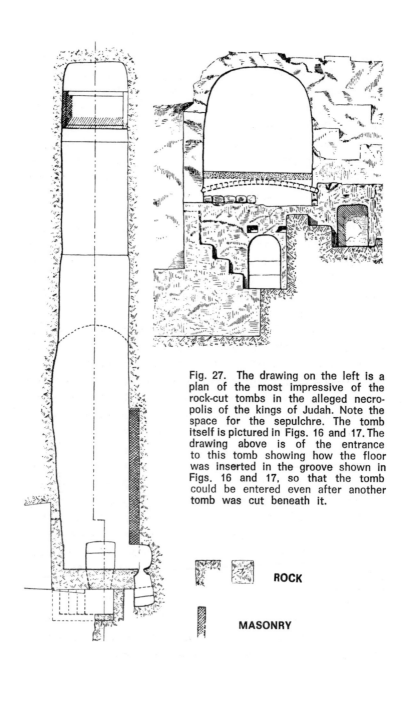

Fig. 27. The drawing on the left is a plan of the most impressive of the rock-cut tombs in the alleged necropolis of the kings of Judah. Note the space for the sepulchre. The tomb itself is pictured in Figs. 16 and 17. The drawing above is of the entrance to this tomb showing how the floor was inserted in the groove shown in Figs. 16 and 17, so that the tomb could be entered even after another tomb was cut beneath it.

ROCK

MASONRY

support across the tomb entrance so that the large upper tomb could be entered even after the lower level tombs were dug (see Fig. 27).

Walk over the rock terracing to the right of these two tombs. There you will see the remains of a large ancient cistern. Some of the plaster is still left on the walls. There are several other cisterns in this excavation area and in one of them Weill found a Greek inscription commemorating the building of a synagogue. The stone on which the inscription is carved is a limestone commonly found in Jerusalem. The text itself, as well as where it was found, indicates that the inscription was probably carved for a Jerusalem synagogue. On epigraphical grounds, both E.L. Sukenik and Clermont-Ganneau have dated the inscription to Herodian times.[47] Because the inscription refers to the grandfather of the inscriber as a synagogue official, it points to the existence of a synagogue in Jerusalem as much as 150 years before the destruction of the Second Temple. This synagogue is therefore the oldest one in Israel for which we have archeological evidence. The inscription reads as follows:

*Theodotus, son of Vettenos, priest and archisynagogus, son of an archisynagogus, grandson of an archisynagogus, built this synagogue for the reading of the Law and for the teaching of the Commandments, and he has built the hostel and the chambers and the waterfittings for the accommodation of those who, coming from abroad have need of them. The foundations of the synagogue were laid by his fathers and by the Elders and by Simonides (Fig. 28).*

Weill also discovered a number of other tombs in this same area. One well-preserved tomb, with a rec-

Fig. 28. The Theodotus synagogue inscription, which dates from Herodian times and points to the existence of an even older synagogue in Jerusalem — indeed, the oldest synagogue in Israel for which we have archeological evidence. The original of the inscription is now part of the permanent collection of the Rockefeller Museum in Jerusalem.

tangular entrance and a magnificent view overlooking the Kidron Valley, is located on the side of the hill (Fig. 29). It can be reached by walking over the rock terracing towards the valley from the smaller of the two tunnel tombs, and taking a narrow rock channel a few steps down the side of the hill. It can also be seen from the tower in the valley, which we now describe.

Down in the valley are the remains of an impressive round tower[48] (see Fig. 30). To reach this tower follow a winding path on the north side of the rock terracing, which begins beside an ancient wall. (This wall, incidentally, appears to be in a line with Nehemiah's wall, although it may be a later reconstruction. We cannot date it with any accuracy because the excavator removed all of the pottery associated with it). The tower is certainly post-exilic and probably Maccabean.

104

Fig. 29. Another tomb in what may be the royal necropolis. This one has a rectangular entrance. It is built on the side of a cliff and has a magnificent view of the Kidron Valley.

Why would anyone build a tower so low in the valley? No one really knows. One conjecture is based on the fact that the bottom of the valley cannot be seen at this point from the top of the hill; even today, one cannot see the road from the tomb area. The tower, according to this suggestion, enabled whoever built the tower to see what was going on in the bottom of the valley.

Jesus refers to a Siloam tower which fell and killed 18 people. These 18, says Jesus, were no less guilty than the other people living in Jerusalem at the time, so the others should beware (Luke 13:4). Some scholars have expressed the view that the tower of Siloam to which Jesus referred is the same as the one we can see today.

Now return to the main road by the path on the crest of the hill from which you came to the royal tombs. On your left, as you return, you will pass the excavations which we noticed on the way up without discussing. These are Weill's excavations of 1923-24. They are tombs, cisterns, and quarries. The tombs lie south of the southern loop of Hezekiah's tunnel, unlike the tombs we have just examined which lie within the southern loop. The tombs you are now looking at therefore led Weill to reject Clermont-Ganneau's theory that the southern loop of Hezekiah's tunnel was taken in order to avoid the area of the royal tombs of the kings of Judah (see "Background", p. 68).

Return to the main road and turn left (north). Walk up the hill to return to the Spring Gihon. On the way — on the right side of the road — is a marvelous Arab bakery located in the basement of a Silwan house. Stop and have some fresh pastry if it is open. Continue your walk up the hill and shortly you will be back at the Spring Gihon.

As I have noted, it is an open question as to whether the tombs we have just looked at, above the southern loop of Hezekiah's tunnel, are in fact the royal tombs of the kings of Judah. One modern authority, David Ussishkin of Tel Aviv University, rejects this identification, but on grounds that are not entirely convincing. Ussishkin has studied some tombs across the Kidron Valley, in the village of Silwan, which he dates between 900 B.C.E. and 750 B.C.E. These, he says, are tombs of Judean nobles (or possibly Phoenician nobles who lived in Jerusalem). According to Ussishkin, these tombs are bigger, more beautiful, and display a higher

Fig. 30. In the foreground are the remains of a round tower that may be referred to in the New Testament as the Tower of Siloam which fell and killed 18 people.

standard of stonework than the alleged tombs of the kings on Ophel. Ussishkin believes it is highly unlikely that these nobles would have finer tombs than the kings; so he rejects the identification of the Ophel tombs as royal[49]. However, even accepting Ussishkin's dates, the nobles' tombs could be later than the Ophel tombs, at which time the Judean nobles could well be building tombs for themselves which surpassed those of the earlier kings.

These Silwan tombs can be seen from the road. Continue up the road past the Spring Gihon between 60 and 80 yards, just past the Cave of Rabbi Ovadya on your right, which the Ministry of Religious Affairs has clearly marked with a sign in both Hebrew and English. Look up the hillside on your right. You will see several square holes in the side of the rock below the level of the houses. The tombs can be entered with the use of ladders. But even from the road, a careful examination of the entrances will indicate that some of these tombs are indeed the last resting place of important personages. Other Silwan tombs can be seen in the village itself by a walk through the main street of Silwan.

# 9 The Spring of En Rogel

Continue — preferably by car — on Siloah Street down into the valley. About seven-tenths of a kilometer from Gihon, past the point where the Hinnom and Kidron valleys meet, is a road on your left, the first road on your left after you leave Gihon. Take this road and park on the other side of a lovely new playground built since 1967. At the corner of the playground is a stone building, behind which are some steps up to the ancient spring of En Rogel. This is all that remains of the spring. However, its waters still richly supply the fields around it, as is obvious from the verdure in almost all seasons. Look back toward Gihon from the playground. You will easily understand why the Jebusites did not find En Rogel an alternative to Gihon as a defensible spring. But En Rogel's location, within shouting distance of Gihon, also makes vivid the story related in 1 Kings 1 of Adonijah's coronation feast at En Rogel occuring at the same time as Solomon's coronation at the Spring Gihon (see "Background", pp. 38-39).

Moslems refer to En Rogel as Job's Well. According to one Moslem legend, Job, in the midst of his misery sat on a dung heap beside this spring. Another Moslem legend has it that a bath in the waters of En Rogel cured Job of his skin afflictions. A third legend has it that God commanded Job to stamp his foot; when he did so a fountain — En Rogel — sprung up for his refreshment.

En Rogel was explored in the 19th century to see if possibly a secret passage led from it to the Temple Mount. Another theory was that an underground river flowed from it. Both proved empty conjectures. In 1847 an English minister descended 130 feet to the bottom of the well and found only rock which had never been worked by a man-made tool[50].

# Notes

1 Ophel means "bulge" or "projection". Originally Ophel referred only to the small bulge just south of the Temple Mount. However, today scholars use the name to refer to the entire eastern spur or ridge.

2 The Tyropoean Valley near Ophel was much deeper — by about 50 feet — and extended farther north in ancient times. In this respect, the topography of Jerusalem has markedly changed in the past 2000 years.

3 This tradition goes back at least to Josephus and probably before.

4 However, it was not until the excavations of 1923—1925 that the archeologists who then excavated on the hill of Ophel could write, "We regard the main question of Jerusalem topography, that of the situation of the 'City of David' as having been definitely settled by our excavation. It was on the Eastern Ridge, between the Tyropoean Valley and the Kidron, not on the Western Ridge, west of the Tyropoean." R.A.S. Macalister and J.G. Duncan, **Excavations on the Hill of Ophel, Jerusalem 1923—1925, Palestine Exploration Fund Annual IV, p. 10.** Even then, a few spectics remained. See H. Sulley, Note, **Palestine Exploration Fund Quarterly Statement,** 1929, p. 124.

5 Although it is commonly supposed that the Jebusites were a Canaanite people, this is by no means the unanimous opinion of scholars. Some believe that although Jerusalem was originally a Canaanite city, it was later captured by the Jebusites who may have been a Hittite people. See, B. Mazar, "Jerusalem Before The Reign of David" in M. Avi-Yonah (ed.) **Sepher Yerushalayim (The Book of Jerusalem),** p. 99 (1956) (in Hebrew). However, for the sake of simplicity and because of the uncertainty surrounding the question, we have acceded to the common assumption that the Jebusites were a Canaanite people who originally built the city.

6 Excavations on the hill of Ophel indicate a settlement here as early as 3000 B.C.E. The name Jerusalem ("Rushulimim") first occurs in Egyptian execration texts dated about 1850 B.C.E. The Jebusite wall around the city dates from about 1800 B.C.E. Jerusalem ("Urusalim") is mentioned several times in the Amarna letters (14th century B.C.E.) as an important Canaanite city. Thus, the name of the city was Jerusalem even before David captured

it from the Jebusites shortly after 1000 B.C.E. The Israelites probably referred to the city as Jebus while it was under Jebusite rule (see Judges 19:10-11 and 1 Chronicles 11:4-5).

7 Another spring (or more precisely, a well), En Rogel, lies south of the eastern ridge (Ophel) beyond its natural defense line. En Rogel would serve the western ridge no better than the Spring Gihon and, as indicated, En Rogel is defensible neither from the western ridge, nor from the eastern ridge.

On the Temple Mount itself, not far from the Gate of the Chain, is what is often thought to be another spring — the Hammam Esh-Shefa. But it is in fact a basin which collects the soil water infiltrating from the neighborhood. It is not a spring.

8 Until recently it was thought that lime plaster was invented in about the 13th century. See W.F. Albright, **The Archeology of Palestine** (Penguin ed. 1949), p. 113. Before that limy marl — a combination of raw lime, clay and sand — was used. Raw lime plaster and even mud plaster cisterns have also been found, as well as occasional rock-cut cisterns.

However, recently lime plaster cisterns have been found as early as the Late Bronze I period (about the end of the 16th century B.C.E.). See Yigael Yadin, **Hazor** (London 1972), p. 39. Why lime plaster was not more widely used until about the time of the Israelite conquest of Canaan is not yet clear. However, at that time hundreds of new sites sprung up in which lime plaster cisterns were used to store water.

The manufacture of lime plaster involves a slaking process by which the lime is burnt and hydrated to form an impermeable plaster.

9 In the story of Judith and Holophernes, recounted in the apocryphal book of **Judith,** the people were collapsing in the streets from thirst after only 34 days, even though there was no question of famine (Judith 7:6-22).

10 Some scholars argue that the well referred to in Nehemiah should be translated the "Jackal's Spring" (see, e.g., the Revised Standard Version). Others contend for the "Serpent's Spring" (see J. Braslavi, "En-Tannin (Neh. 2:13)", **Eretz Yisroel,** Vol. 10, p. 90 (1971) (in Hebrew; summary in English). The identification of this biblical reference with En-Rogel needs re-examination (see J. Braslavi, op. cit.).

11 At least this is the view of the excavator, Kathleen Kenyon. Others question whether this wall could have been used for a thousand years. If so, it would be the first such wall known.

According to Miss Kenyon, in the 8th century, this wall was replaced by another wall just in front of the Jebusite wall. All trace of this later wall has disappeared. The wall seen directly behind the Jebusite wall is the last wall built before the Babylonian destruction of Jerusalem in 586 B.C.E. Above this wall are modern terrace walls.

12 Some scholars have recently expressed the view that what is commonly thought to be the Jebusite watershaft was built by an Israelite king. These as yet unpublished views rely on the fact that similar water systems dating from the Israelite period have been excavated at Megiddo, Gibeon and Hazor. One problem with this theory is that another similar water system, at Gezer, is dated by W.G. Dever, the archeologist in charge of the recent re-excavation at Gezer, to the Late Bronze Age, or more specifically, c. 1550—1400 B.C.E. See Dever, "The Water Systems at Hazor and Gezer", **The Biblical Archeologist,** Vol. 32, p. 71 (1969).

13 Biblical scholars argue about the meaning and intention of almost every word of the text, including the lame and the blind, already referred to. In rabbinical tradition, the lame and the blind were not men, but Jebusite idols placed on the walls of the city.

According to a more modern interpretation based on Hittite parallels, the Jebusite reference to the blind and the lame was not a taunt, but a curse. Anyone who touched the lame and the blind posted on the walls would be cursed. According to this interpretation, Joab was the first to smite one of these and thereby establish that the curse was ineffective. Y. Yadin, **The Art of Warfare in Biblical Lands,** pp. 267-270 (London 1963).

14 Professor W.F. Albright, who, until his recent death in 1971 was the dean of biblical archeologists, has described the sentence in which "tsinnor" appears as "one of the most difficult exegetical problems in the historical books of the Old Testament". "The crux of the difficulty", he says, "is the obscure word 'sinnôr'." W.F. Albright, "The Sinnôr in the Story of David's Capture of Jerusalem", **Journal of the Palestine Oriental Society,** Vol. 2, p. 286 (1922).

15 This meaning is supported by E.L. Sukenik, W.F. Albright and Y. Yadin. E.L. Sukenik, "The Account of David's Capture of Jerusalem", **Journal of the Palestine Oriental Society,** Vol. 8, p. 12 (1928). The most recent suggestion based on Ugaritic, Hattite, and Akkadian parallels is that "tsinnor" means drum, the idea being that the "tsinnor" was a drum used as a psychological weapon in the same way that Joshua used his trumpets at Jericho. M.

113

Dietrich and O. Loretz, "Zur Ugaritischen Lexikographie I", **Bibliotheca Orientalis,** Vol. 23, p. 127, at p. 132 (1966). However, the suggestion does not appear to fit the biblical text.

16 L.H. Vincent, **Underground Jerusalem — Discoveries on the Hill of Ophel (1909-1911),** p. 34 (London 1911).

17 Note that according to the account in **Samuel** the city was taken simply by the "King and his men" (2 Samuel 5:6), i.e., by the king's immediate cortege, rather than by his sizable standing army. This further supports the conclusion that it was by some ruse relating to the watershaft that David was able to subdue the city.

18 The Samuel text states that "David built around (the city) starting at the Millo". The word Millo is always written in Hebrew transliteration rather than translated. Its meaning has been something of a mystery. Scholars are agreed that etymologically Millo means filling. But they find it difficult to go beyond that point, although suggestions, many of them quite bizzare, have been rife. Some have suggested that the filling was a defensive mound or tower. Others have suggested that it refers to a rampart on the northern border of the city which was not defended by a natural valley. One difficulty with this suggestion is that there are references to re-building the Millo long after the city expanded northward when the northern wall of the City of David would no longer be the crucial northern wall of the city. In that event, there would be no need to continue to repair the Millo.

Recent excavations on the eastern slope of the eastern ridge have revealed a series of terraces with huge retaining walls on which houses were built. In this way, the early inhabitants of the city were able to use the steep eastern slope of the eastern ridge. Obviously these terrace walls and the fill which made a level area behind the retaining walls had to be kept in repair. Many archeologists agree with Miss Kenyon, who excavated the remains of these terraces and first put forth the suggestion, that this system of terraces — literally "fill" — is what is meant by Millo. In times of destruction, disuse and disrepair, much of the Millo and the houses on them collapsed.

19 Some scholars believe that the seige of Jerusalem (described in 2 Kings 18:17-19:35) came not in 701 B.C.E. following Sennacherib's ravaging of the cities of Judah, but rather as a result of a second refusal by Hezekiah some 13 years later to pay tribute to the Assyrian king. See John Bright, **A History of Israel,** pp. 267-271; 282-287 (Philadelphia 1959).

20 "Vain and worthless is the help of Egypt", the prophet had said (Isaiah 30:7. See also Isaiah 19, 20, 30:2-3, 31:1-3). According to the theory put forth in the preceding footnote, however, Isaiah supported the second refusal to pay tribute and predicted that the Assyrians would not be able to enter Jerusalem (see 2 Kings 19:32).

21 See also Isaiah 10:16.

22 See Note 9 above.

23 The Jebusite shaft was apparently no longer in use or was not considered adequate to the needs of an expanded and enlarged city.

24 That it continued to be regarded as one of the wonders of the ancient world is reflected in the fact that it is referred to again in the apocryphal book of **Ecclesiasticus:**
Hezekiah fortified his city, bringing water within the walls. He drilled through the rock with tools of iron and made cisterns for the water. (Ecclesiasticus 48:17).

25 It has been estimated that the tunnel took about eight months to construct. L.H. Vincent, **Underground Jerusalem,** p. 23 (London 1911).

26 The word which I have translated "split" and, alternatively, "overlap" is in Hebrew זדה. It is clearly the most difficult word in the inscription. It has not yet been successfully connected with any Semitic root. Albright, Sayce and others relate it to "excess" or "overlap". More commonly, it is translated as "crack" or "fissure" or "split", not for any philological reason, but, as one commentator has pointed out, simply because this seems to fit "the context moderately well". W.A. Wordsworth, "The Siloam Inscription", **Palestine Exploration Quarterly,** 1939, p. 41.
See also Frank R. Blake "The Word זדה in the Siloam Inscription", **Journal of The American Oriental Society,** Vol. 22, p. 55 (1901).
Mrs. Amiran uses the translation "crack" as a major support for her argument that the serpentine path of the tunnel can be accounted for by the fact that the tunnelers were following a crack in the rock from Gihon to Siloam. See note 34 below.

27 Note for antiquarians only: There is some confusion in the literature as to who found the inscription. Captain Warren reported in 1884 that it was found by "some Jewish boys who were attempting to go through the tunnel". **(The Survey of Western Palestine —Jerusalem,** Vol. III (1884), p. 346). From this account it has often been repeated that the inscription was found by some Jewish boys.

(See, for example, Sarah K. Fox, **Footloose in Jerusalem** (1970), p. 117). On the other hand, Clermont-Ganneau, the French archeologist, reported that the inscription was found by some Arab boys bathing in the Pool of Siloam. **Lés Fráudes Archéologique en Palestine,** p. 16 (Paris 1885). From this, it has often been repeated that the inscription was found by Arab boys. See, for example, Jerry M. Landay, **Silent Cities, Sacred Stones** (1971), p. 227. The account of the discovery of the inscription in the October 1880 issue of the **Palestine Exploration Fund Quarterly Statement** is by Conrad Schick who states: "A short time ago, one of my pupils, when climbing down the southern side of [the tunnel], stumbled over the broken bits of rock and fell into the water. On rising to the surface, he discovered some marks like letters on the wall of rock". "Phoenician Inscription in the Pool of Siloam", p. 238. The author of the article, Mr. Schick, was a scholar who reported copiously on Jerusalem excavations until his death in 1901. He was also a Protestant missionary. The school he operated was for Jews, as part of his missionary effort for the London Mission to the Jews. In 1951, Bertha Spafford Vester, of the family which for years led the American Colony, an American relief and missionary group in Jerusalem, reported that the boy who found the Siloam inscription was born Jacob Eliahu. His parents .had been Sephardic Jews from Turkey, but Jacob, although born in Palestine, was a student at Mr. Schick's school. Jacob and his family became some of the first converts of the London Mission to the Jews. Mrs. Vester is in a position to know the story because at age 17, a year after he found the inscription, Jacob came to live with the Spaffords at the American Colony, and in 1883 was formally adopted by them. Later he took the name Jacob Spafford. Mrs. Vester describes in detail the effort Jacob and a companion made to explore the tunnel and how Jacob found the inscription. (Bertha Spafford Vester, **Our Jerusalem (1951),** pp. 100-101). The only apparent inaccuracy in her story is her description of the finding of the writing at the place where the two crews of workmen met. The inscription was not carved in the middle of the tunnel where no one could see it, but at the high-ceilinged outlet near the Pool of Siloam. However, it does appear from several contemporaneous accounts that the inscription was found by a student at Mr. Schick's school and the likelihood therefore is that the student who actually discovered it was Jacob Eliahu, who, at the time, had already converted to Christianity.

28 Charles Warren and Claude R. Conder, **The Survey of Western Palestine** — Vol. III, **Jerusalem,** pp. 355-6 (London 1884).

29 According to one story, the same young man who earlier discovered the Siloam inscription (See note 27, above) convinced
members of the Parker Mission, whom he met socially, to request
Père Vincent to record scientifically the results of their explora-
tions. Bertha Spafford Vester, **Our Jerusalem**, pp. 225, 230 (1951).
According to another account, it was Père Vincent who approached
Captain Parker because the former was disturbed at the fact
that so important an excavation would not be properly recorded.
Père Vincent requested permission to follow Capt. Parker's
excavations and promised absolute secrecy. So impressed was
Captain Parker with Père Vincent's presentation that he granted
the permission. Le Père Lagrange, **Au Service de la Bible**, p. 195
(Paris 1967). The latter version seems more consistent with Père
Vincent's own reference to a letter of introduction which he had
to the head of the expedition. **Underground Jerusalem**, p. 1 (London
1911).

30 When King Zedekiah fled from Jerusalem during the Babylonian
destruction, he tried to escape by night through a gate near
the King's Garden which is referred to as the "gate between
the two walls" (2 Kings 25:4). This also suggests a second wall.

30a. In the original publication of this wall, "Excavations in the
Jewish Quarter of the Old City of Jerusalem, 1970", **Israel Exploration Journal**, Vol. 20, p. 129 (1970), Professor Avigad showed only
one angle, the northern one. The second angle, which turned up
on subsequent digging, was published in "Excavations in the Jewish
Quarter of the Old City", **Qadmoniot**, Vol. 5, Nos. 3-4, 1972 (in
Hebrew), (which issue did not actually appear until March 1973)
and in the **Israel Exploration Journal**, Vol. 22, No. 4, p. 193 (1972)
(which did not actually appear until April 1973). For some reason
which is not entirely clear, in the **Qadmoniot** and second IEJ
article Professor Avigad places the main north-south portion of
the projected wall considerably further to the west than he does
in his article in the **Israel Exploration Journal**. This not only
emphasizes that the location of the north-south projection of this
wall is not determined by the part that has been excavated (see
following footnote), but also highlights the conjectural nature of
Professor Avigad's map locating the wall. Yigael Yadin has
suggested that Avigad's wall might be a separate wall enclosing
the western hill only, with no connection to the wall enclosing
the hill of Ophel. See note 14 of Professor Avigad's first IEJ article.

31 This newly discovered wall is also of great significance in
fixing the date of the city's expansion to the western ridge. In

short, there was some expansion of the city to the northeastern part of the western ridge in the pre-exilic period. Thus the new wall proves wrong both the minimalists — who contended that Jerusalem did not expand to the western ridge during the pre-exilic period — and the maximalists — who contended that the city covered the entire western ridge in the pre-exilic period.

Professor Avigad's new "map" has by no means been unanimously accepted by scholars. None of the lines of Avigad's map which carry the wall south are determined by the angle of the wall itself. Problems obviously remain, and substantial excavation is obviously called for.

32 The rock appears to be harder in the northern part of the tunnel, which accounts for the slower progress of the northern crew, and softer and less compact in the southern part of the tunnel, as evidenced by the eroded caves, ledges, faults and holes in the southern half of the tunnel. Thus there would seem to be no geological reason for the southern crew to turn so quickly east and to continue in this direction even after they had found soft rock, rather than turn north. The northern crew dug west instead of south, despite the hard rock in the northern part. On the other hand, Père Benoît of the Ecole Biblique et Archéologique Française has pointed out to me that in general rock in Jerusalem becomes softer at the same level as one progresses southeast. See L.A. Picard, "Geology" in M. Avi-Yonah (ed.) **Sepher Yerushalayim (The Book of Jerusalem)** (1956) (in Hebrew); see also M. Hecker, "Water Supply of Jerusalem in Ancient Times" in op. cit. A few geological soundings might provide a definitive answer to these speculations.

33 M. Clermont-Ganneau, **Les Tombeaux de David et Des Rois de Juda et le Tunnel-Aqueduc de Siloé** (Paris 1897).

34 Ruth Amiran has recently suggested the theory that the tunnelers simply followed a crack in the rock through which water seeped from Gihon to Siloam. R. Amiran, "The Water Supply of Jerusalem", **Qadmoniot**, Vol. 1, No. 1, p. 13 (1968) (in Hebrew); If it were true, we would not expect the twistings and turnings and false starts at the point where the tunnelers were attempting to effect a meeting of the two halves. Moreover, the unusual height of the tunnel in the southern half, especially near the Pool of Siloam, also seems to me a difficulty with Mrs. Amiran's theory. This unusual height resulted from a lowering of the floor after the tunnel was joined in order to get the water to flow down-

ward from the Spring Gihon to the Pool of Siloam. If there had been a crack in the rock through which water had flowed and which had come out where the Pool of Siloam was to be located, the southern crew would have started digging at the level of the crack, not at a level many feet higher which would require a lowering of the floor when the tunnel was completed. Among those who have read the manuscript of this book, Dan Bahat and Père Benoît reject Mrs. Amiran's theory. However, Yigael Yadin believes it is the best solution proposed thus far.

35 "The king's garden" was probably adjacent to the original pool at the time of the Babylonian destruction of Jerusalem. At that time, King Zedekiah sought to effect an escape by night through "the king's garden" (2 Kings 25:4; Isaiah 39:4; 52:7).

36 But cf. J. Simons, **Jerusalem in the Old Testament,** p. 191, n. 1 (Leiden 1952).

37 However, prior to Hezekiah's time, Isaiah had his famous encounter with King Ahaz at the "end of the conduit of the Upper Pool" (Isaiah 7:3). Therefore the "Upper Pool" may be a reference to Gihon, where the waters were collected in an open basin. The encounter took place at the end of the Solomonic channel.

38 It is also called the Fountain of the Steps.

39 In the last century, it was believed that the waters of Siloam were a sure cure for rheumatism and many people bathed in its waters hoping to cure their rheumatic complaints.
Moslems believed that bathing in the waters of Siloam would cure fever. However, the bath had to be taken on Friday during the midday prayer, after which the waters of Siloam were poured over the patient seven times. See T. Canaan, **Mohammedan Saints and Sanctuaries in Palestine,** pp. 110-111 (London 1927).

40 See Kenyon, **Jerusalem,** p. 19 (1971). Although Macalister found that the tower was originally built by David, he called it a Solomonic tower because of a supposed re-building by Solomon. R.A.S. Macalister and J.G. Duncan, **Excavations on the Hill of Ophel, Jerusalem, 1923-1925,** Palestine Exploration Fund Annual IV (London 1926), plate facing p. 49.

41 Macalister regarded this tower as post-exilic. R.A.S. Macalister and J.G. Duncan, **Excavations on the Hill of Ophel, Jerusalem, 1923-1925,** Palestine Exploration Fund Annual IV (London, 1926), pp. 49-50. According to Miss Kenyon, this tower cannot be precisely dated. It could have been constructed anytime from the 5th century B.C.E. onward. Kenyon, **Jerusalem,** p. 114 (1971).

42 The importance of these homes destroyed in the Babylonian devastation of Jerusalem is reflected in the fact that as late as 1962, the most widely used textbook on biblical archeology was lamenting the fact that "From Jerusalem no archeological evidence of the Babylonian destruction has been recovered". G.E. Wright, **Biblical Archeology,** p. 182 (rev. ed., Philadelphia, 1962). Miss Kenyon's excavations make this statement no longer true.

43 The bastion was a strengthening of a weak point in the wall. It was underground from the time it was constructed, so it could not be used to storm the wall.

44 This Solomonic channel forks at the end. The exposed exit is the less important one. Another exit, now underground, is about ten feet west of the exposed exit.

45 Although Weill, who excavated this channel, regarded the part beginning at the iron gate as a continuation of the Solomonic channel, Vincent believed this part of the channel was added by Ahaz and that the Solomonic channel went off just before this point into the valley. Vincent and Stève, **Jérusalem de l'Ancien Testament,** p. 645 (Paris 1971). However, both Weill and Vincent agree that up to this point the channel is Solomonic.

46 This part of the channel was also used by Hezekiah as part of the outflow channel from the Pool of Siloam. Since Hezekiah wanted it to flow in the opposite direction, he lowered the floor. The lower part, where the channel is narrower, was dug by Hezekiah; the upper, wider part was dug by Solomon (so Weill) or by Ahaz (so Vincent).

47 E.L. Sukenik, **Ancient Synagogues in Palestine and Greece,** p. 69 (London 1934) and S.A. Cook, "The Synagogue of Theodotus at Jerusalem", **Palestine Exploration Fund Quarterly Statement,** 1921, p. 22.

48 Just east of the tower, further in the valley, is an entrance to a portion of the Solomonic channel. The channel itself is unfortunately blocked.

49 Ussishkin, "The Necropolis from the Time of the Kingdom of Judah at Silwan, Jerusalem", **The Biblical Archeologist,** Vol. 33, p. 34 (1970).

50 G. Dalton, "The Exploration of En-Rogel or Job's Well", **Palestine Exploration Fund Quarterly Statement,** 1923, p. 165.

# Jerusalem Chronology

c. 3000 B.C.E. —

Earliest discovered remains of habitation at Jerusalem on the hill of Ophel.

c. 1850 B.C.E. —

Jerusalem ("Rushulimim") referred to in Egyptian execration texts.

c. 1800 B.C.E —

The Jebusites build the wall of Jerusalem which was not excavated until 1961.

c. 1350 B.C.E. —

Jerusalem ("Urusalim") referred to in Amarna letters, diplomatic correspondence written in cuneiform Akkadian and discovered in Tell el-Amarna, Egypt.

c. 1000 B.C.E. —

David becomes king.

c. 993 B.C.E. —

David captures Jerusalem, seven years after becoming king. Jerusalem becomes the City of David and the capital of the country.

c. 961 B.C.E. —

Solomon anointed king at the Spring Gihon.

c. 922 B.C.E. —

Solomon dies and his kingdom is divided into the kingdom of Israel and the kingdom of Judah.

722 B.C.E. —

The kingdom of Israel falls to the Assyrians.

c. 715—687 B.C.E. —

Hezekiah is king of Judah.

701 B.C.E. —

The Assyrians, after destroying much of Judah, lay seige to Jerusalem. The seige is unsuccessful and the kingdom of Judah is saved.

586 B.C.E. —

Jerusalem is destroyed by the Babylonians. The kingdom of Judah comes to an end.

c. 445 B.C.E. —

Nehemiah rebuilds the walls of Jerusalem, builds a new wall on the east side of Ophel higher up on the slope.

70 C.E. —

Jerusalem is destroyed by the Romans.

135 C.E. —

The Romans build Aelia Capitolina establishing the present lines of the city walls of the old city of Jerusalem. Jews are forbidden to live in Aelia Capitolina.

1535 C.E. —

Suleiman the Magnificent builds the presently-existing wall around the old city of Jerusalem.

1967 C.E. —

The old city of Jerusalem enclosed by Suleiman's wall and the ancient City of David on the hill of Ophel become part of modern Israel.

## CHRONOLOGY OF EXPLORATIONS
## ON THE HILL OF OPHEL
## (THE CITY OF DAVID)

**1838**

Edward Robinson is the first man in modern times to traverse Hezekiah's tunnel.

Edward Robinson. *Biblical Researches in Palestine, etc. — A Journal of Travels in 1838* (London, 1841).

**1864, 1867**

Charles Warren, Charles Wilson and Claude R. Conder in the course of their survey of Jerusalem for the newly-formed Palestine Exploration Fund explore and survey Hezekiah's tunnel and discover the Jebusite shaft.

Charles Wilson and Charles Warren. *The Recovery of Jerusalem* (London 1871).

Charles Warren. *Underground Jerusalem* (London 1876).

Charles Warren and Claude R. Conder. *The Survey of Western Palestine — Jerusalem,* Vol. III (London 1884).

**1886**

Conrad Schick explores the Solomonic irrigation channel leading south from the Spring Gihon along the eastern slope of the eastern ridge.

Conrad Schick. "The Aqueducts at Siloam", *Palestine Exploration Fund Quarterly Statement*, 1886, p. 88; "Second Aqueduct to the Pool of Siloam", *Palestine Exploration Fund Quarterly Statement*, 1886, p. 197; "The 'Second' Siloam Aqueduct", *Palestine Exploration Fund Quarterly Statement*, 1891, p. 13.

## 1894—1897

F.J. Bliss and A.C. Dickie conduct new excavations on Ophel and examine the remains of the Byzantine Church above the Pool of Siloam.

F.J. Bliss and A.C. Dickie. *Excavations at Jerusalem 1894—1897* (London 1898).

## 1909—1911

The Parker Mission searches for the original manuscript of the Law of Moses and the Ark of the Covenant; in the course of the search, Hezekiah's tunnel and the Jebusite shaft are cleared, and Père L.H. Vincent writes a full description of the underground water systems.

L.H. Vincent. *Underground Jerusalem — Discoveries on the Hill of Ophel (1909—1911)* (London 1911) (translated from the French).

## 1913—1914; 1923—1924

Raymond Weill discovers tombs above the southern loop of Hezekiah's tunnel. Weill believes they are the royal tombs of the kings of Judah; he may be right.

Raymond Weill. *La Cité de David* [Paris 1920 (Vol. I) and 1947 (Vol. II)].

## 1923—1925

R.A.S. Macalister excavates a massive fortification tower the lowest courses of which he dates to King David's time. The tower promptly becomes known as the Tower of David. It later turns out to be a Maccabean tower of the 2d century B.C.E.

R.A.S. Macalister and J.G. Duncan. *Excavations on the Hill of Ophel, Jerusalem, 1923—1925.* Palestine Exploration Fund Annual IV (London 1926).

1961—1967

Kathleen M. Kenyon discovers the Jebusite city wall and finds 7th century B.C.E. Israelite homes below Macalister's so-called "Tower of David". She also places the western Jebusite city wall so that the Pool of Siloam is unaccountably outside the city.

Kathleen M. Kenyon. "Excavations in Jerusalem, 1961—1967" *Palestine Exploration Quarterly,* Vol. 94, p. 72; Vol. 95, p. 2; Vol. 96, p. 7; Vol. 97, p. 9; Vol. 98, p. 73; Vol. 99, p. 65; Vol. 100, p. 97 (1962—1968).

1970

N. Avigad discovers a new fortification wall probably built by Hezekiah which he believes enclosed the Pool of Siloam.

N. Avigad. "Excavations in the Jewish Quarter of the Old City of Jerusalem, 1970" *Israel Exploration Journal* Vol. 20, p. 129 (1970).

---

Not included in this list are the excavations and explorations of Clermont-Ganneau (1873), Guthe (1881), and Crowfoot and Fitzgerald (1927—1928), because no major remains of their work can be seen today and no reference to these scholars has been made in the text. The excavations at the south wall of the Temple Mount being conducted since 1968 by Professor Benjamin Mazar of the Hebrew University have not been included because they are not as yet in the City of David.

# Suggested Further Reading

Kathleen M. Kenyon.
*Digging Up Jerusalem*, London, 1974.

Kathleen M. Kenyon.
*Jerusalem — Excavating 3000 Years of History*,
n.p. 1967

Kathleen M. Kenyon.
*Royal Cities of the Old Testament*, London, 1971

J. Simons.
*Jerusalem in the Old Testament*, Leiden, 1952

L.H. Vincent and A.M. Stève.
*Jérusalem de l'Ancien Testament*,
Paris, 1954 (Vol. I) and 1956 (Vol. II)

*Jerusalem Revealed, Archaeology in the Holy City, 1968-1974*,
Jerusalem, 1975.

"Jerusalem", *Encyclopaedia Judaica*, Jerusalem, 1971

# List of Illustrations

Fig. 1. Entrance to the Spring Gihon    16

Fig. 2. Rock contours of Jerusalem, showing the present old city walls, with Mount Zion and the hill of Ophel projecting southward    21

Fig. 3. The Jebusite wall of Jerusalem built in about 1800 B.C.E.    24

Fig. 4. Reconstruction of the ancient gate leading to the Spring Gihon    25

Fig. 5. Plan and section of the Jebusite shaft and tunnel system    28

Fig. 6. Plan of Jerusalem during King David's time    33

Fig. 7. View inside the Jebusite tunnel    34

Fig. 8. Detail of relief from Sennacherib's palace at Ninevah showing Hebrew captives impaled on Assyrian spears    41

Fig. 9. Cuneiform prism recounting Sennacherib's campaigns in Judah    45

Fig. 10. View inside Hezekiah's tunnel    50

Fig. 11. Plan of Hezekiah's tunnel    52

Fig. 12. The Siloam inscription    56

Fig. 13. Edward Robinson, 19th century explorer of Palestine    58

Fig. 14. Newly-discovered fortification wall dating from King Hezekiah's time, found in the old city of Jerusalem    65

Fig. 15. Plan of Jerusalem in King Hezekiah's time    67

Fig. 16.   View of ancient tomb in the City of David,
           possibly belonging to a Judean king          70
Fig. 17.   View looking out of the tomb pictured in
           the previous illustration                    71
Fig. 18.   Superimposed plan of Jebusite shaft and
           tunnel system, Solomon's irrigation chan-
           nel and Hezekiah's tunnel                    73
Fig. 19.   The landing leading to the Spring Gihon     78
Fig. 20.   Overview of the eastern slope of the City
           of David                                     80
Fig. 21.   Tunnel leading to blocked-up entrance of
           Jebusite shaft                               83
Fig. 22.   Maccabean tower thought by its excavator
           to date from King David's time               85
Fig. 23.   Remains of 7th century B.C.E. houses
           destroyed in the Babylonian destruction
           of Jerusalem                                 87
Fig. 24.   View looking up Jebusite shaft              91
Fig. 25.   View of the Pool of Siloam from a 19th
           century engraving                            96
Fig. 26.   Necropolis and Roman quarry in the City
           of David                                     100
Fig. 27.   Plan of ancient tomb, possibly belonging
           to a Judean king                             102
Fig. 28.   Theodotus synagogue inscription             104
Fig. 29.   View of ancient tomb overlooking the
           Kidron Valley                                105
Fig. 30.   The tower of Siloam                          107

## Illustration Credits

Zev Radovan photographed the cover pictures and Figs. 1, 3, 9, 13, 16, 17, 19, 20, 21, 22, 23, 26, 29 and 30; David Harris photographed Figs. 8 and 12; Peter Clayton photographed Fig. 2; Avinoam Glick photographed Fig. 14.

Figs. 8, 9, 10, 12, and 28 are by courtesy of the Israel Department of Antiquities and Museums; Figs. 7 and 24 are by courtesy of the Ecole Biblique et Archéologique Française, Jerusalem; Fig. 2 is by courtesy of the Palestine Exploration Fund, London; Fig. 14 is by courtesy of N. Avigad and the Institute of Archeology, the Hebrew University of Jerusalem.

Fig. 4 is by Brian Lalor; Fig. 5 is after L. H. Vincent and K. M. Kenyon; Fig. 6 is after K. M. Kenyon and N. Avigad; Fig. 11 is after L. H. Vincent; Fig. 15 is after N. Avigad; Fig. 18 is after R. Weill; Fig. 13 is from C. R. Conder, Palestine; Fig. 25 is from C. Wilson, Jerusalem the Holy City; Fig. 27 is from L. H. Vincent in the Revue Biblique.